TERNI

TO

TEHERAN

The Life and Times Of a Pilot

LES WARREN

PREFACE

Les was just 17 when he applied to join the RAF to train as a pilot. This story follows his training to the award of his 'wings', through his squadron life flying the Canberra twin jet bomber, his time as a qualified flying instructor and to his eventual command of a 747 'Jumbo' in British Airways.

I dedicate this book to my grandchildren who only know me as their grandad and have very little idea of my life before they were born.

Les Warren

Amazon Kindle Edition

CONTENTS

Flying?

So, there I was. Last term at school and no idea what I was going to do for a living. I had been at my boarding school for seven years and managed, mostly, to keep out of trouble. I had learned fairly early on to keep my head down to avoid any flak and it had seemed to work, but now I had to make some sort of a decision which would probably affect the rest of my life.

I was in my second year sixth form and had just taken my A levels in Physics, Chemistry and Biology. The Biology was a cop-out because I just wasn't good enough at Maths, the obvious choice for anyone taking Physics. I reckoned that I could probably scrape a pass in Biology with minimal work, and so it turned out as it was the only pass I achieved.

My Chemistry result was dire, and I just managed to scrape a failure in Physics. However, because I had only *just* failed Physics A level, I was awarded a pass at O level. A shame really as I already had two passes at Physics O level – one because I had taken it as Physics-with-Chemistry at O level two years before and another one because after one year in the 6th form, and studying Physics at A level, I was awarded another O level pass having taken it as 'practice' for next year's A level. I would happily have traded two of them in for Maths!

The only certainty at this point of my life was that I couldn't see any career in Physics, Chemistry or Biology that would hold any interest for me. I think that is probably why I had difficulty in getting down to serious study in the 6th form. Now, as the end of term loomed, I had to get my mind around the next 40 or 50 years.

In 1958 career advice at the school was non-existent. There was, I had just discovered, a small room near the Headmaster's office where there were a few books and pamphlets on various careers for school leavers. I dragged myself in there with zero expectation.

I picked up a pamphlet on flying as a pilot in the RAF. I think what probably attracted me was the picture on the front of a young man in flying gear standing next to a jet – really cool! I also remembered cycling down to Dunsfold aerodrome from the school one weekend with one of my friends and, from the boundary, seeing one of the new shiny black Canberras taking off which I found really exciting. That must have lodged somewhere in my mind.

Reading through the blurb inside the pamphlet I became interested when I found I had all the qualifications to apply for 'Pre-Assessment'. I had the necessary five O levels, including English and Maths, and was seventeen and a half years old (minimum) and, best of all, I would get three days off school to attend the Aircrew Selection Centre at RAF Hornchurch in Essex. Where do I sign?

I was pleasantly surprised when the school agreed to release me for the three days in the middle of term after I had an acceptance letter from the RAF to attend their Selection Centre. It was, after all, no big deal as I had taken all my exams and was only clicking my heals until they threw me out onto the streets. Even if I had failed miserably with the RAF the three-day pass was not to be sniffed at.

Selection

Off to Hornchurch then! Train from Witley station to Waterloo with a couple of hours in the cartoon cinema on Waterloo station as I had time to kill. I was enjoying my new career already. Then the Tube to Hornchurch on the District Line.

I soon found myself checking into the Selection Centre with quite a few other young men, some of whom looked considerably older and more worldly wise than me. This was undoubtedly because the upper age limit for selection was 25. Some of these men had obviously been employed for the last few years and it showed. I was beginning to feel just a little bit inadequate.

There must have been around 60 of us for this particular assessment and it seemed to me that 59 of them had wanted to be pilots since they were two years old whereas I had only thought about it since last week!

We had an introductory welcome from a senior RAF officer who outlined the programme for the next three days. There would be written tests to see if we were literate and numerate; aptitude tests to see if our limbs and eyes were connected in the right order; medical examinations to see if we had, indeed, the correct parts working as they should, and tests to see if we had the necessary leadership qualities, to mention just a few.

Before embarking on the programme, we all had to change into boiler suits which we would wear for the next three days so that the manner of our dress would not influence the examiners. We were split into teams and kept to those groups for the duration of our time at the Centre.

At one stage we were taken to a hanger and each member of the team, in turn, was designated the leader and given a (sometimes impossible) task for his team to perform: for example, trying to cross a fast, crocodile infested river marked out on the hangar floor without losing any members of your team. To help us we were given a pole (too short) and a piece of rope (?). I guess the purpose was to ascertain your leadership and organisational qualities, not necessarily whether you managed the task allotted.

Another 'game' was to get a large, heavy barrel onto the roof of a shed with assorted pieces of useless equipment – I don't know whether anybody ever achieved that.

There were various paper exercises where you, as a team, had to work out a knotty problem. For example, how to cross a desert in a Land Rover with limited fuel and various stops, each of which presented problems. This seemed to be a variation of trying to get the fox, the goose, and the hay across a river in a boat without the fox eating the goose or the goose eating the hay, etc.

During the three days there were various interviews where you were questioned in close detail, which is where I thought they might discover how little I knew about the RAF or aeroplanes. They did ask me why I had not joined the Combined Cadet Force or the Air Training Corps whilst I was at school. I could quite honestly tell them that my school didn't cater for that, but I had to do some fast thinking when the questions got around to aeroplanes! I will never know whether they were impressed with the depth of my knowledge or my ability to avoid answering the questions.

As far as the aptitude tests were concerned, I remember the small black and white TV with the randomly moving spot which you had to keep in the small square in the centre of the screen using a joystick. The machine would measure the number of times you let the spot drift out of the square. There were obviously various levels of difficulty programmed into it because, as time went on, it became more and more difficult to keep the spot in the centre.

One of the written tests showed a series of pictures of an aircraft artificial horizon and you had to determine whether the aircraft was climbing or descending, turning left, or turning right and any combination of different attitudes. Gamers today would walk it!

At one of the daily sessions, we were invited to stand in front of an audience of the other would-be-aviators and give a talk on any subject of your choice for 15 minutes or so. Normally I think this would have freaked me out, but it just so happened that I had been asked by our Physics master at school that term to give a talk on 'Extra Sensory Perception' to the Science Society. He had given me a book on the subject to help me prepare and it had gone quite well, even though I thought ESP was a load of baloney. I tweaked it a bit and brought it down to the 15 minutes and used that. I think everybody else gave talks on aviation!

At the end of each day about a third of the candidates were invited to 'go home' and I have to admit that I was more than a little surprised to find I was still there each following day. I would have put money on some of the guys dismissed as being eminently suitable to end up as Air Chief Marshalls. You just never can tell.

The medicals were thorough, as you would expect. As well as general medical fitness there were comprehensive hearing and visual tests, colour blindness being a big no-no.

One hearing test which amused me was where you stood at one side of a room with the doctor at the opposite wall. You faced 90 degrees away from him and he whispered words which you had to repeat whilst his assistant pushed his finger in your ear furthest from the doctor and moved it about trying to drown out the doctor's voice. If you had been determined to fail, you could have had a lot of fun with that one!

At the end of day three we were dismissed for home, or in my case, school. It had been an interesting few days and I left having absolutely no idea how I had performed but fairly laid back as I had no expectations. I can only imagine the stress involved if flying in the RAF had been the only thing you had ever wanted to do.

ITS, South Cerney

At the end of term, and in my case the end of formal education, we departed for home and the summer holidays. I would kick my heels for a while, ride my bike and try to earn some money with a part-time job locally. I felt no particular pressure to research a career as I had already set the ball rolling in aviation: that was what I told my anxious parents. However, as the weeks went by and I had heard nothing from the RAF I began to feel a little twitchy about my prospects.

By late August I had decided that I would really have to write to the Air Ministry and ask them, as I had obviously been unsuitable, why they could not have had the good grace to send me a formal rejection so I could get on with my life.

In the end I did, in fact, tone it down a little and asked them, if it were not too much trouble, how I did at Hornchurch, if they could remember me.

I was amazed the following week to receive a letter from the Air Ministry, with a scrappy looking attachment listing the clothing I should take and sports equipment, for the sports I intended to pursue, with instructions to make my way to 'Cirencester, Gloucestershire by train (Travel Voucher enclosed) to arrive in the afternoon of Thursday 25th. September where the train would be met by RAF transport to take you to the Initial Training School at RAF South Cerney.' Our induction ceremony

into the RAF would take place on 27th September 1958, and our course would start on the Monday.

Let me say straightaway that if I had been gainfully employed in the outside world for a few years and had now arrived on day one of my RAF career, South Cerney, or the ITS (Initial Training School) as it was known, would have come as a great shock to me. For a start we were accommodated in large dormitories with about 20 cadets (as we now were) in each. We each had a tall locker and an iron single bedstead. In fact, everything I had come to know and love for the last 7 years at school. My transition to the adult world would be quite seamless it would seem. The only difference was the terminology: we were now living in a barrack block.

There was a senior officer, a Squadron Leader, in charge of our 'squadron' of cadets and this squadron was split into two 'Flights', each flight being led by an RAF Flight Lieutenant. Now this was really beginning to feel like the Airforce.

On our first evening we were assembled at the foot of our beds and our squadron leader, with our flight commander, introduced themselves and inspected our clothing to see if we were fit to be young budding RAF officers.

I was quite taken aback when the 'boss' told me that the brand new navy blue raincoat, with a rather tasteful shot silk lining which I had hanging in my locker, was quite unsuitable as it made me look like an off-duty policeman. He even inspected our grooming kits and told us that, in future inspections, he would not want to see any hair on hairbrushes!

On 27th we were duly sworn into the RAF by a senior officer. It was a bit like joining the Cubs, but without the 'Dib, Dib, Dib.' We had a form to sign acknowledging the fact and including a form detailing the Official Secrets Act which we also had to sign. We were issued with a service number which would stay with us for life.

We were now officially employed and were loyal servants of the Queen. Pay was £5 per week but food, accommodation and uniform were included. As I said, just like school.

On the Monday morning we were marched off to the Clothing Stores to be fitted with a uniform and to pick up all the associated paraphernalia, boots, webbing belts, hats, etc. We had walked from A to B for the last time – we now 'marched' everywhere.

I was a bit confused when the camp tailor, who was an elderly civilian gentleman, looked at me and called out a size over his shoulder to an assistant. An officer's number 1 uniform jacket was passed to me which I tried on – perfect! The tailor then proceeded to draw chalk marks all over the jacket where he obviously intended to make (quite unnecessary) alterations and directed me to hand it back. I discovered later that his bonus was based upon the number of alterations he had to make!

We were each issued with two webbing belts: one covered in a shiny blue polish and another in white blanco. In my case I had two blue belts. I pointed out their mistake and was told that I would have to make one of the blue belts white with the tin of blanco supplied, after first removing *all* the blue polish!

We would have white flashes on our collars and white discs behind the badges on our berets to distinguish us from the ordinary airmen on the station and to let everybody know we were Officer Cadets. This made no difference in practice as our ranks were the lowest in the RAF – AC2 (Aircraftman 2nd class).

Each day we would have lessons each heavily weighted towards aviation, naturally, and exams to look forward to at the halfway point in what we now knew to be a three-month course.

During this time, we would be taught to march and instructed on everything associated with being on a parade ground. We had each been issued with a .303 Lee Enfield rifle which, when not being used on a parade ground or on the Firing Range, would be bolted to the iron frame of our beds. It was never to be out of our sight whilst not locked onto the bed and we were mindful that the UK still had the death penalty!

For the first week we spent an inordinate amount of time either on the parade ground or, if the weather was inclement, in a hangar, learning which was our left foot and which our right. We learned how to salute and to whom and all the manoeuvres one can complete with a rifle.

We thought things were a little over the top when we found ourselves being taught fairly complicated funeral drill with the rifles, morning, noon, and night (literally) until we found out that one of the staff pilots on the station had killed himself on a training flight in the station Chipmunk aircraft. We were to be the funeral party the following weekend! A baptism of fire.

One incident sticks in my mind to this day. We were all assembled at the foot of our beds ready for the usual kit and personal inspection by the boss, waiting for him to finish his inspection in the upstairs dormitory.

Just then a cadet came thundering down the stairs and threw a pair of shoes through the door of the Barrack block onto the grass. This was followed a few minutes later by another cadet launching a pair of shoes through the door.

All the while we could hear raised voices from upstairs and then the air seemed to be filled with shoes passing our windows, thrown from upstairs onto the grass below!

It seemed that today the boss was having a crackdown on dirty or worn shoes. Any cadet whose shoes didn't come up to muster was told to throw them out! We waited in trepidation for our turn. Our boss seemed to have either bad days or worse days and he seemed to target a particular item for each inspection. His favourite was hairbrushes. He was always accompanied by his two large dogs who seemed to be as frightened of him as we were. He would hold a hairbrush up to the light and if he saw any hair on it would throw it onto the bed and shout that he "wouldn't brush my dogs with that."

At that time in the late 50's the Cold War was really beginning to ramp up and so we had our fill of films about the effects of nuclear blasts and the subsequent radiation and we were taught how to use a dosimeter to check the level of radiation and to wear the appropriate gear.

We had a splendid team of instructors, most of whom were gnarly old NCO's (non-commissioned officers) who had been around since the RAF were flying biplanes made of string and canvas. They had a marvellously grounded way of putting over their subject, full of very descriptive swear words and obviously believing that they were teaching adults and not schoolboys. This was balanced by the more gentlemanly approach of some of our officer instructors teaching subjects like Air Law and the structure of the RAF.

We noticed that virtually all our instructors wore an aircrew brevet, or wings. The officers tended to be pilots, navigators, or air electronic officers and the NCO's air gunners and observers: all hugely experienced.

As would-be pilots we would be going into the General Duties branch of the RAF which meant, as its name implies, that we could be called upon to perform any type of duty from flying aeroplanes to 'flying' a desk. Our instructors at South Cerney had obviously spent at least one flying tour (each usually two and a half years) and were now fulfilling a 'ground' tour.

At the halfway point of our course, we took exams on all our subjects and then spent a few days at 'camp'. In our case this was up in the Brecon Beacons in Wales. Getting there was going to be interesting. We knew we were going on a camp but had been given no details.

We were assembled in a briefing room at 6pm one evening, dressed in boiler suits and had been told to bring four pennies (that's 4d not 4p). At the briefing we were told that we were expected to be on parade at the camp up on the

Beacons at 8am the following morning. We were supplied with a map and the map reference of the camp.

Once we left the briefing room we were not to follow or talk to each other but were to make our own way to the map reference by whatever way we could without breaking any laws.   The four pence were so that we could make an emergency phone call from a phone box (remember them?) should it become necessary.

The first obvious conclusion was that the Brecon Beacons were at least 80 miles from South Cerney as the crow flies, so walking was not an option. With fourpence we couldn't buy a train ticket, nor could we nick a bike (no breaking the law). That really only left hitch hiking, and who was going to be driving up into the Beacons on a cold, wet night? We weren't even allowed to travel in groups for company.

The briefing finished with the briefing officer wishing us goodnight and hoping to see us in the morning at camp.

We piled out into the night trying not to go in the same direction as everybody else but as we were all going to the same place anyway this was going to be difficult. It reminded me of the post war POW escape films we had all dosed up on in the 50's.

After what seemed like a hell of a long time, I managed to flag down a truck going in approximately the right direction and, as I hefted myself over the tailgate into what was obviously a farm vehicle, another couple of cadets appeared and jumped in beside me. So much for not making this a joint effort!

We spent a long and less than comfortable ride until the driver stopped somewhere near the base of the Brecon Beacons and invited us to leave. It was now late, and we were cold, tired, and hungry but we pressed on.

After about three hours it became obvious that we weren't going to make camp in the dark as we had very little idea of where we were, so we decided to bed down for what remained of the night. We were by a stream and, to hell with the instructions, we cuddled together to conserve what little warmth we had.

That must have been one of the most uncomfortable nights I have ever spent anywhere but there was no danger of oversleeping or, indeed, of sleeping at all.

Come the dawn we gathered ourselves together and set off in what turned out to be the right direction for the camp. We didn't actually make it by 8am but it was a close-run thing.

The camp consisted of several large tents, a cooking area where we were delighted to smell breakfast cooking, and an assembly area with a flagpole, at the top of which fluttered the RAF ensign. This had been raised on the parade at 8am in a ceremony known as the 'Flag Wag' which we had failed to attend! Our Squadron Leader, Flight Commander, and various members of the ITS instructors would be at the camp for the duration.

The next few days were spent taking part in various leadership, shelter building, map reading and general boy scout type games, not to mention cooking and washing up. The days were fairly full and exhausting and the nights cold and damp but mercifully short!

Really the only thing which sticks in my mind after all these years is a night exercise in map reading where we had to find and decipher messages hidden around the route. To this day I can remember two of the messages: - "Pas d'elle yeux rhone que nous" ("paddle your own canoe" – get it?) and the other:- "Un petit, d'un petit, c'est en eval". Of course, "Humpty Dumpty sat on a wall".

Naturally, our time at the camp was punctuated by mini parades and numerous kit inspections which had become our way of life anyway so that was no great hardship.

We were all pleased, not to mention relieved, when we struck camp at the end of the week and were transported by

RAF trucks back to South Cerney and dismissed after a debriefing.

It was Friday evening and we had been given a pass to go home for the weekend; the only time for the whole course when we would escape the RAF. However, we had been instructed to be on parade in our full uniform and boots at 8am on Monday morning.

I made my way home to Dartford in Kent where my family was living at that time. My stepfather had been in the army for many years and, when I told him that I had to be on parade on the Monday morning with shining boots, which I had worn all through our camping sojourn and knocked the hell out of, he stepped up to the plate.

"Give 'em to me, lad, I'll fix 'em!".

He then spent most of the day cleaning them up with 'spit-and-polish' until I could see my face in them wherever I looked.

I can tell you that on the parade on Monday morning I could have had leprosy: nobody wanted to stand next to me with those boots on. Even the inspecting officer asked me if they had been the boots I had taken to camp. To add insult to injury I was held up as an example to the rest of the Course! I was obviously a 'beastly swot.'

The rest of the day did not go so well. We each had interviews with the 'boss' to discuss our progress over the course to the halfway point, specifically the results of our exams.

I had failed one of the papers (can't even remember which one) and so I could not continue. In mitigation the pass marks were extremely high, around 80%, but I knew that so there was no excuse. Normally at this point one would expect to be dismissed the ITS and given the option to remain as an ordinary airman in another branch of the RAF or to leave the Service as a civilian.

To my surprise the Boss, who normally gave no quarter, said that my dad, who he knew had been a Sergeant Major in the army, would 'Kick my arse,' and so he was going to give me another chance by re-coursing me to the next course. Dismiss!

More of the same now. I joined my new course who were several weeks behind my original intake and settled in fairly well. I did not look forward to another camp at the halfway point but, hey, I had done it all before, so it held no surprises.

This time I passed all the halfway exams and we cadets now moved into the Officers' Mess for the second half of the course to learn how to live as an officer.

I progressed uneventfully to the end of 'term' and the finals. I was determined not to fail this time and so it was that in February 1959 I received a posting to No.6 Flying Training School at RAF Ternhill in Shropshire for my basic flight training. We would get to fly the RAF's standard initial trainer, the Piston Provost.

My commission as an Acting Pilot Officer was activated on 10th February, my 18th birthday, and the youngest point at which I could hold a commission. I could then say that, however briefly, I was the youngest officer in the RAF! This acting rank would apply for a year, after which I would become a substantive 'Pilot Officer' if I had progressed satisfactorily to that point.

6 FTS, Ternhill

Ternhill had a reputation amongst trainee pilots as being the harshest of the Basic Flight Training Schools. It came as no surprise then that on the evening of the day of our arrival we were assembled in the ante room of the Officers Mess for a welcome and introductory briefing by our new Flight Commander, an extremely young-looking Flight Lieutenant. By way of an introduction to no. 148 course, as we now were, he said that we would assemble outside the mess at 6am the next morning dressed in our sports gear, shorts and tee shirts, when we would be taken on a run around the airfield by the PT corporal.

On assembly we were to present to the officer in attendance copies of our complete life history which we would write that evening in the comfort of our own rooms. So, this was how they treated young APO's!

Suffice it to say it was a hoax. The course in front of us was a university intake and they had dressed up the most distinguished looking candidate on their course in the Flight Commander's uniform to give us our 'welcome'. No wonder he looked young. However, we didn't find out we had been conned until, on that freezing and dark winter's morning, over the other side of what seemed to be a very large airfield, a car drove by, picking up our 'corporal' and driving off at speed, the occupants laughing and whooping and leaving no. 148 course at first confused and then annoyed that we had been well and truly had.

The flying course at Ternhill would last about nine months. During that time, we would accumulate about 120 flying hours and end up reasonably proficient at operating the aircraft and would be prepared for moving on to the advanced stage of flying on a jet aircraft.

Throughout the course there would be several flying tests at each stage of progress ending up with a 'final handling test'. It was obviously necessary to pass each flight test to the appropriate high standard.

In parallel with the flying there was also a comprehensive ground school syllabus to be covered in all subjects associated with flying as an RAF pilot, even the Morse code! We did, however, unlike ITS, manage to get most weekends off and were free to leave the station to go home or to spend time in the local area.

We were split into Flights of about fifteen students per Flight. I was in D Flight and was given the callsign of 'Delta Charlie' which would remain with me for the whole course. Each flight would have its own crew room where we would spend down time and each had a respectable coffee bar, dartboard, and assorted board games where we could amuse ourselves between flying sorties. Outside we had volleyball nets for the physically active.

Each of us had a regular instructor who had, typically, three students. Most of the flights were taken by your regular instructor but there were changes from time to time and flying tests were taken by another staff pilot, probably the Flight Commander or other senior instructor. Each sortie would last about 45 minutes and would be 'full on'. In fact, the only leisurely trip was the first one – flight familiarisation - where you weren't expected to do anything, just enjoy the ride, and overcome the novelty of being in the air. After this the work really began.

The expectation was that between 10 and 15 hours you would be ready to fly your first solo. 10 hours was good but if you approached 15 hours without having flown solo you were subject to close scrutiny and in danger of failing the course and leaving the RAF. It was a sobering thought that within two to three weeks from the start of flying you could be piloting the aircraft on your own, even if, as in a lot of cases, you had never flown before.

I can well remember being overawed at the complexity of the controls and the instruments and wondering if I would ever come to terms with it but it was introduced to you piecemeal and it all fell into place.

Before your first solo you had to be competent not only in taking off, flying round a circuit at the airfield and landing safely but also in performing a forced landing into a field should the engine fail.

During the pre-solo stage there were also lessons on entering and recovering from a spin! Although, frankly, if you got yourself into a spin on your first solo circuit you were just not ready!

My first solo was at a relief airfield, High Ercal, close to Ternhill, which was not busy and so ideal for inexperienced students. I had performed three fairly respectable take-offs, circuits and landings and my instructor, a young Flying Officer by the name of 'Titch Clarke' on his first instructional tour, said,

"OK, Warren, stop the aircraft here in front of the tower and I will get out. I've had enough so you can do this next one on your own. Remember, if you don't like your approach to land, just put on the power and go round and try again. No problem."

When he got out and slid the canopy closed, I don't think I had ever felt so alone in all my life. The instructor's seat looked *very* empty.

I took my time and performed my pre take-off checks (out loud!) and, with permission from the tower for the very first time, 'Delta Charlie' taxied out to the take off point. Whilst flying dual you always used the instructor's callsign, so this was the first airing of 'Delta Charlie'.

The take-off was good, the climb to one thousand feet at circuit height also uneventful. I made my radio call

"Delta Charlie, downwind for landing".

I Proceeded with clearance after my "Finals" call and shortly thereafter decided that I didn't like my alignment to the runway and so made the call,

"Delta Charlie, Overshooting," and applied the power, proceeding to fly the circuit all over again.

The second time I landed with no problem and taxied round to the tower to pick up a very worried looking instructor. As he climbed in he tried to sound casual as he asked why I had decided to go round again.

"Well, I had done better, so I decided to give it another go, as you suggested".

I remember the date well – 16th March 1959 – five weeks after my arrival at Ternhill and 16 days since my familiarisation flight.

With the solo hurdle out of the way we now settled down to the rest of the course.

There was a rather unpleasant incident about halfway through the course. One of our youngest instructors had struck some power cables whilst teaching a low flying exercise in the Provost. Both he and his student were unharmed, but the aircraft was damaged, and a few hundred homes were left without power. This was a profoundly serious offence, and he was Court Martialled.

He was charged by the court with recklessly descending below his minimum safety height of 250 feet above ground level and thereby negligently damaging one of Her Majesty's aircraft by flying through power cables which were 29 feet above ground level.

His defence was that he had started by demonstrating to his student what 250 feet agl (above ground level) looked like, then took the aircraft up to 350 feet to show a 'too high' situation, followed by the 'too low' case which is where the accident occurred.

Frankly, he was clutching at straws as there was no way that it was necessary to fly that close to the ground, whatever the demonstration.

His other students were called as prosecution witnesses and they would testify under oath that he did, with them, fly frighteningly low.

Character references were presented but he was found guilty and dismissed the Service.

It was a great shame as he was an extremely popular and competent pilot but, in the view of the court, had demonstrated that he lacked the necessary judgement to be an effective QFI. It was purely by chance that he didn't kill himself and his student. Several of us on the course had to attend the court as 'officers under instruction' to show us the way a military court martial operated. As General Duties Officers we could well have been called upon at any time to sit on a Board of Enquiry or to act as a defence or prosecution counsel at a court martial.

During my time at Ternhill we had covered a very comprehensive syllabus including stalling, spinning, forced landing practice in case of engine failure, instrument flying, navigation, aerobatics, formation flying and various types of instrument approaches to the runway.

The final navigation test was one which I remember very well and had not been looking forward to.

I had been scheduled to fly it with 'Delta Zulu', one of our notorious examiners who was a lovely, friendly man on the ground but a strict tyrant in the air.

I had to plan to depart from Ternhill, to fly to a first waypoint; in my case this turned out to be Rhyl on the north Welsh coast. From there I would have to set course to a second waypoint, a small village, and finally to a small lake in the middle of Wales. After this we would fly back to Ternhill.

The pre-flight planning would have to be done using the latest winds from a meteorological forecast which I had to pick up from the Station Met Office. I was not told the location of my first waypoint until we were walking out to the aeroplane and, having strapped into the machine, I was given five minutes to come up with a time and heading, correcting for estimated wind, for Rhyl.

What made the exercise particularly tricky was that I had to fly the first sector with an opaque instrument hood over my helmet so that I couldn't see the ground to see how I was doing. If my flying on instruments was not accurate, my mental arithmetic was poor, or the actual wind was not as forecast, then, when I raised the hood from my helmet I would not be where I would hope to be.

However, I was relieved to see the town beneath us when I removed my hood but then had a couple of minutes to come up with a heading and time for the next waypoint. Trying to fly the aircraft whilst fiddling with a large map and a pencil, all the while applying estimated winds to the new track to come up with a heading, I found very tricky, not helped by an obviously impatient examiner next to me.

Eventually we set off for our second waypoint which I managed to identify some distance off to one side of our track but after setting off for our last point, there was no expected lake and I, frankly, was a bit thrown by this. My instructor was less than helpful when he said,

"OK, Columbus, where are we?"

He took control and rolled the aeroplane onto its back and, pointing at the ground, which was now above our heads, said,

"What's that town down there, and where's the lake?"

Hanging from my straps, I mumbled something whilst I was scrabbling to retrieve my map and pencil from the top of the canopy of our inverted provost and he, impatiently handing back control to me, asked me what our bearing was from Ternhill.

By this time, I had already decided that I must have failed this one and had a stab at,

"Two Six Zero degrees, Sir."

"Well," he said, "Call for a true bearing from the tower at Ternhill."

"True bearing, true bearing, Ternhill tower this is Delta Zulu requesting true bearing."

"Delta Zulu, this is Ternhill tower, your true bearing is two six zero degrees."

I cannot describe the look on the instructor's face as he tried to hide his amazement. It was almost as 'gobsmacked' as mine must have been.

"OK, Warren, give me a time and heading for base and let's get back."

I scraped a pass on that one! On the plus side I made Rhyl and then the village, but god only knows where the lake got to! It had been a hot, dry summer so maybe the water had evaporated!

My 'Final Handling Test' on 29th September 1959 was conducted by a Squadron Leader from another Flight and it went quite well. That, effectively, was the end of my basic flying course and I was ready to progress to jets.

It was a sobering thought to realise that a little over a year ago I was still at school. Somehow, I managed to fit in driving lessons during the summer evenings and at the weekends and passed my driving test at Whitchurch, a little town in the north of Shropshire. Couldn't afford a car yet, though.

5 FTS, JETS!

We were given a couple of weeks leave at the end of our ITS before our arrival at No. 5FTS at RAF Oakington, near Cambridge, late in 1959. We would be flying the RAF advanced jet trainer, the Vampire T11, a dual seat training version of the single seat Vampire which had been one of the RAF's first jet fighters in the early 50's.

As I arrived at Oakington there were two or three Vampires flying circuits around the airfield. These were being flown by students of earlier courses and there was an unmistakeable smell of kerosene in the air, a smell which would stay with me for the whole course.

The members of our course, number 145, were accommodated in the overflow section of the Officers' Mess, a selection of huts near to the main mess building. They were comfortable enough and we each had a room to ourselves looked after by a batman shared with several other students.

Our batman was an elderly gentleman, ex-military from way back, and he would keep our rooms tidy, clean our shoes and bring us a cup of tea in the morning before breakfast in the main mess building.

A light tap on the shoulder with, "Your tea, sir: Seven o'clock and a lovely sunny day."

This was the life! Definitely nothing like school. I must admit to feeling a little awkward being called 'Sir' all the time by a lovely old gentleman old enough to be my grandfather. As far as he was concerned, we were Pilot Officers, however young, and nothing was too much trouble for him.

I was really looking forward to flying the vampire even though I knew it was going to be a tough course. As at Ternhill, we were split into Flights and a small number of our students were going to be flying the Meteor rather than the vampire because they were too tall for the cockpit of the T11.

The vampire, with its two side-by-side ejector seats, was tight on space and we each had to be measured for thigh length to see if we could safely eject from the aircraft in an emergency without our knees hitting the metal frame of the canopy! This was to be our first experience of sitting in ejector seats and would require complete familiarisation of the equipment.

The use of ejector seats was made necessary since the war due to the ever-increasing speed of military aeroplanes. It was found to be almost impossible to jump out of a fast-moving aircraft in trouble due to the slipstream pushing you back into the cockpit. Once ejection was initiated the process was completely automatic.

The seat contained explosive charges which would propel you upwards out of the cockpit and then, through an automatic sequence, would release you from the seat, and when clear, would deploy the parachute. All this could happen even if the pilot were unconscious.

Being on jets we would now be operating well above the height limit for flight without oxygen and so would be using oxygen masks for all flights.

Life on the flight line was similar in many respects to Ternhill. We had the usual crew room with coffee bar and each instructor had three or four students.

We would start off with the very pleasant familiarisation when we could get all our "Oohs, and Ahs," out of the way and then straight into the meat of the course.

The vampire did really feel like your own personal rocket ship. The performance compared with the basic trainer Provost was astounding! As soon as you were off the ground you raised the undercarriage (the wheels) and they tucked away neatly into the wings and the view ahead was spectacular as the jet engine was behind you, unlike the Provost which had a large engine cowl in front restricting your view. Everything happened at a much higher speed and was therefore going to be more challenging.

We would expect to fly between 110 to 120 hours over the next nine months or so at the end of which, dependent on making the grade, we would have earned our 'wings' – the brevet that every RAF pilot wears on his left breast.

My instructor was a United States loan officer, Captain Bill Eldridge, a veteran of the Korean war. He came from the deep south of the USA so, not only did I have to learn to fly the vampire but also had to learn to understand what he was saying.

When he was ready to send me on my first solo, he, very touchingly, walked around the aircraft as I sat in it with the engine running seeming to inspect it minutely before giving me the 'thumbs up' and beaming broadly as he sent me on my way.

Unlike the provost, this first solo consisted of more than just a circuit and landing. This time you had to leave the circuit traffic and fly around the local area before returning to re-join the pattern for a landing. In all, about thirty minutes. I had the distinct impression that the jet was flying me not the other way round, but it was very exhilarating.

One alarming exercise which we had to master was entering a spin from high altitude, around 30,000 feet, and recovering from the spin by 15,000. It was a little worrying because, on the recovery manoeuvre, the vampire would, for a couple of turns, speed up its spin before suddenly coming out.

The briefing was that, if the aircraft was still spinning by 12,000 feet, despite recovery action having been taken, the instructor would give the order for the student to eject and would then eject himself at 10,000 feet.

Over the years there had been a significant number of accidents involving spinning vampires and so it was to be treated with respect. Towards the end of our course one of our instructors had been killed after he failed to eject from a spin, for reasons unknown, after his student had ejected safely. The student landed in his parachute unharmed.

This was not our only fatal accident on the course. A fellow student, Joe Ball, just a couple of weeks from gaining his wings, had taken off on an instrument rating exam where he had an opaque 'hood' mounted on his helmet so that he could only see his instruments. After take-off he was instructed to turn onto a particular heading whilst climbing and the vampire collided with an RAF transport aircraft that was flying through the area. Both aircraft crashed and both Joe and his instructor were killed as were all the occupants of the other aeroplane. Jo would not have seen anything as he was under the instrument hood.

There were, of course, some very enjoyable highlights of the course. I enjoyed immensely doing aerobatics and formation flying, both exacting but very satisfying. Another real fun pursuit was a tail chase. A leading aircraft would climb and dive, perform various aerobatic manoeuvres, weave around clouds whilst two or three other jets, in 'line astern', would have to follow the leader's every manoeuvre.

At about this time I was feeling the lack of having a set of wheels to try out my driving skills and to bring the delights of Cambridge within my scope. I was not flush for cash but another student on my course was selling his 1938 Morris 8 for £50 and I could just about manage that. Although it was three years older than me it seemed to be in good condition, if a little short on modern niceties. A further £8 would cover the road tax for the year and insurance would see off another fiver or so. A little over £60 would get me on the road.

I have to say that being able to see the road through the floorboards in the front of the car was a little alarming and the air rushing past your legs in cold weather made you regret the lack of any heating but, hey, this chariot had a soft top and how cool was that?

It was about this time that I discovered that Beryl, a young lady from my class at school, was at Girton College in Cambridge. She had a very nice friend, Gillian, a vicar's daughter as I remember, and, with a friend of mine on our course, we made up a foursome to gad about in Cambridge.

My friend had a splendid motor car – a Triumph Roadster which was open topped, had two seats in the front and two 'dickie seats' behind, which was like a boot opening revealing the two seats. The four of us arriving anywhere in this would always turn heads.

As we approached the last week of the course, we were all scheduled to take our 'Final Handling Test'. This was the big deal and would cover anything and everything we had learned about operating the vampire, and not only the vampire but flying as a responsible and fully alert pilot in the RAF.

A successful completion of this test would mean we would be awarded the coveted RAF Flying Badge (our wings) and could move on to converting onto the type of aircraft we would be operating on a front-line squadron.

Towards the end of the course, we had been asked by the Squadron Commander to indicate our choices of the types of aircraft we would like to fly operationally. This was taken into account when we were awarded our postings to the Operational Conversion Unit (OCU), but the final decision would also depend on how we had performed on the course as well as our suitability for a particular role.

The choices in those days were, Fighters, Bombers, Transport, Coastal, Helicopters or back into Training Command as an instructor (what we called 'creamed off').

Throughout the flying training, both basic and advanced, several trainees had fallen by the wayside, failing to measure up to the required standard. There were now eleven of us left out of an original twenty or so who turned up at Ternhill and we would be awarded our wings on a passing out parade to take place in August of 1960.

We had now been given our future postings to an OCU where we would convert to the type we would fly on our first squadron. I was destined to go to RAF Bassingbourne, close to Cambridge, where I would learn to fly the twin engine Canberra bomber and team up with my new crew of two navigators. Now, after several years I would be flying the aircraft that had so impressed me as a schoolboy when I saw it taking off from Dunsfold. Who would have thought? Certainly not me!

My course at Bassingbourne would not be starting until early November and so the RAF had to decide what to do with a young, newly winged, pilot officer. I was posted down to RAF Biggin Hill to help arrange the Battle of Britain open day and air display for that year. I was a general dogsbody called upon to do anything and everything.

One of the popular attractions was the ejector seat demonstration ramp. It consisted of a steeply upward sloping rail which would guide the seat from ground level to about thirty feet. The 'pilot' would be strapped into the ejector seat and, on drawing the safety blind down over the front of his face, the seat would fire and be propelled, with its occupant, upwards, extremely rapidly, to the top of the rail. Obviously, this was in the days before any meaningful 'health and safety' rules. It was supposed to mimic the action of ejection from a jet.

Initially, it would require an experienced volunteer to be the first to demonstrate it. This would be me!

I can clearly remember as I unstrapped myself from the seat, having been wound down to ground level again, a young boy approached me and said, "Cor, Mr. You a pilot?" I tried awfully hard to look nonchalant.

231 OCU, CANBERRAS

O n arrival at 231 OCU, RAF Bassingbourne, there were three pilots, including myself, from my Vampire course at Oakington. We attended a reception with all the pilots for '195, Long Bomber' course. All the other pilots were experienced aviators converting from their previous squadrons on different types of aircraft and so were older, and certainly more experienced, than we three babies with our shiny new wings.

At the reception we met the navigators who would team up with the pilots. The navigators had, from their navigation courses, already paired off and were now just looking to find a suitable pilot to make up the team. I was approached by two navigators who had decided that I looked a reasonable candidate for their crew, so the deal was done! Jimmy Milne, who would be my nav. plotter, was nine years my senior, as indeed was Brian 'Digger' Balding who would be my nav. observer, or bomb aimer.

I was interested to find out that they had both started their careers in the RAF as trainee pilots but, for whatever reason, had not made the grade and had been given the option to change to a navigation course. This, I found out later, was far from unusual. In fact, it was generally easier to find a failed pilot in a nav's seat than one who had made navigation his first choice. From then on, all our flying would be together as a crew.

The first ten hours or so I flew were on a Canberra T4, the trainer version of the B2, which had two pilots' seats, side by side. This was similar to the single pilot B2 but had some handling differences, amongst other things. During this initial instruction I had to familiarize myself with not only operating a different, much larger, aeroplane but also how to fly a twin-engine aircraft with all the asymmetric problems which would be experienced if an engine failed.

When my instructor was happy to let me loose on the single pilot B2 he poked his head through the side entrance door whilst I was sitting in the only pilot's seat and pointed out the differences in the instrumentation and talked about the handling differences I would encounter. Meanwhile, my two twenty-nine-year-old navigators sitting behind me, tried to look as though they were entirely confident with their nineteen-year-old pilot flying this aircraft for the first time.

The briefing was to take off, leave the circuit for a brief reconnaissance of the local area and then return for a final landing. However, on our return to the airfield for our landing we experienced a partial hydraulics failure which meant that I could not lower the flaps.

The flaps change the wing shape enabling the aircraft to approach the runway at a lower speed, a different angle and therefore use less runway for landing.

With our 'flapless' approach the runway at Bassingbourne was too short and so I would have to divert to an airfield with a longer runway. This was Marham, in Norfolk. This would be no big deal: the approach angle would be flatter than usual and the landing run longer but the runway at Marham was plenty long enough to deal with this and so we diverted.

My instructor, who was waiting patiently for us to return, wondered where on earth we had got to when we didn't land back at Bassingbourne.

After the first few hours with an instructor on the T4 working our way through all the exercises necessary to become entirely happy with flying the Canberra, we started to concentrate more and more on flying the B2 with our normal crew in more operational flying.

There would be long, high level navigation exercises, up to three hours at a time, to fly over three or four waypoints around the British Isles, sometimes in a well separated stream with other Canberras, occasionally giving UK fighter squadrons the opportunity, having seen us approaching on radar, to try to intercept us.

It has to be said that this was more of an exercise for the navigators than for the pilots as, apart from the fact that the Canberra had no autopilot, all the pilot had to do was to fly the aircraft as accurately as possible whilst following the navigator's instructions. It could be fairly mundane, especially at night.

It did become more interesting when we flew the occasional bombing sortie over some of the UK's bombing ranges. We would only be dropping 8lb practice bombs, but that would be the same as dropping a larger bomb only causing a much smaller explosion. It would be enough to see how close you were to the target.

This was where the Nav. Bomb Aimer came into his own. He would normally be sitting in his ejector seat next to the Nav. Plotter, both behind the pilot and separated from him by a bulkhead. When the aircraft was within range of the target the bomb aimer would unstrap from his seat and, passing the pilot, would crawl along a short tunnel into the nose of the aircraft where the bombsight was mounted in a clear plexiglass nose cone. He had excellent forward and downward vision.

Approaching the target, he would tell the pilot that he was ready and, with his thumb on the bomb release button, would give the pilot 'left' and 'right' commands to line up accurately for the run-in. Approaching the target, the pilot would open the bomb doors and continue to fly as accurately as possible taking the bomb aimer's commands. These would become faster as the aircraft approached the bomb release point, typically,

"Left...Steady, Steady...Right..Steady...St e a d y" until the bomb aimer pressed the release button,

"Bomb Gone!"

He would now stretch forward and, looking down through the nose cone, could see if the bomb was falling away from the aircraft,

"Bomb Falling, Bomb Doors Closed!".

The bombing range was observed from a couple of points on the ground so that the bomb strike could be accurately plotted for use in debriefing after the flight.

Over time the crew would get to know one another and the relationship between the pilot and the bomb aimer would develop. The pilot would become familiar with interpreting the increasing speed of the instructions from his bomb aimer and would understand how small an adjustment to make.

Even in the sixties this was second world war technology and relied on many variable factors for accuracy, unlike the guided weapons of today. Not only was it necessary for the bomb aimer to talk the pilot into accurately lining up the aircraft with the target but the pilot had to fly accurately with no slip or skid and so rudder control was critical. The estimate of the wind at the release altitude needed to be fed into the bombsight which was a basic analogue type computer and this wind would have been supplied by the nav. Plotter. Any errors would influence the falling bomb. All in all, it was a wonder we managed to get anywhere near the target! Still, we now were beginning to feel as though we were an operational crew and of some use to the RAF.

Although we still flew a lot during daylight most of the operational type flying was flown at night. This could be a bit of a problem at Bassingbourne where winter fog could be frequent and it wasn't at all unusual to hear the station tannoy announcing around 5pm that, "Night Flying for tonight is cancelled."

It was on such an occasion that the responsibility of the Captain of the crew was brought forcefully home to me.

We had had a few consecutive nights where we had been completely fogged in and consequently had not flown. On the morning after one such night my nav. bomb aimer had arranged some sort of appointment for the coming evening in London. He told me that he had squared this with the Flight Commander who had agreed to release him but anyway, he said, owing to the fog he felt that our chances of flying were slim.

In the event, that night was crystal clear, and we were going to take full advantage of the weather to get in a full programme of flying.

On the way to the briefing room, I was told by another pilot that my bomb aimer had had his request for time off rescinded owing to all the cancellations of flying we had experienced. This was news to me but, as I knew that tonight was a navigation exercise only, I did not need the bomb aimer and we could operate quite well with just the one navigator.

In the briefing room the Squadron Commander started the ball rolling by saying, "Captains, answer for your crews," and then read out each pilot's name to get a, "Present" answer.

After my acknowledgement I was immediately approached by my Flight Commander who was obviously ready for this.

"Where's Balding?"

"Er, I dunno, but we don't need him as it's nav only."

"Tell him to report to me first thing tomorrow morning, and you be there too".

At breakfast the next morning 'Digger' Balding, my bomb aimer, asked if we had flown the previous evening.

"Yes, it was a lovely evening, and we are both wanted in the Flight Commander's office at 9am sharp."

"Christ," he said, "I'd better put on my best uniform."

We were wheeled into the Flight Commander's office and immediately told to follow him into the Squadron Commander's office.

The Squadron Commander asked Digger why he went to London when he had expressly been told not to. Digger politely declined to answer, whereupon the four of us filed into the Wing Commander Flying's office.

After a couple of further embarrassing questions from the WingCo we arrived at our final destination: The Station Commander's office.

We were now in the presence of the High Priest, the man in charge of RAF Bassingbourne, sitting at his impressive desk with Digger and I stood in front of him and his three deputy executioners sitting either side of him. If it hadn't been for the fact that we were in deep trouble it would have been very amusing, a bit like a Brian Rix farce.

The Station Commander was known to be a bit ineffectual and we waited, stood to attention in silence, whilst he gathered his thoughts. His first question was the one we had heard several times already that morning,

"Now then, Balding", he said, looking at a piece of paper on his desk which obviously had Digger's name on it,

"Where on earth were you last night which was more important than your primary duty, flying in the Royal Air Force?"

Digger realised that the game was up, and he would have to come clean about his absence.

"Well sir, I am a Freemason and hold a high position in this particular lodge and had been requested to attend a meeting."

There was an embarrassed silence (at that time many senior officers in the forces were Freemasons) and you could almost hear the whirring of the cogs in the Station Commander's brain. He didn't quite know what to do but he had to put on an impressive show of command.

As he went into a badly rehearsed tirade, accentuated by his thumping the desk, he spluttered,

"Well, B...Baldock", now frantically looking for the piece of paper with Balding's name on it which his flailing fist had blown to the floor,

"This just isn't good enough and I have no option but to give you three extra Orderly Officer duties, and to warn you not to try this trick again."

This was too much for Digger who found that being punished with the lightest punishment possible when he was expecting to be thrown off the course was the funniest thing he had heard, and forthwith started to snigger. Looks of horror all round whilst the Station Commander decided that the safest way to extricate himself from this situation was to move his attention to me.

"And you, Pilot Officer Warren, as captain of your crew, should be in a position to know where they are at all times. I hope you have learned from this. Now dismiss!"

We saluted and the five of us filed out wondering what all that had been about.

The rest of the course was quite uneventful after that, and we progressed towards our final handling test at the end of February 1961.

Earlier that month, On 10th February, I was promoted to Flying Officer from Pilot Officer which was automatic after one year as Acting Pilot Officer and a further year as Pilot Officer. I had now been commissioned for two years and it wasn't quite two years since my first solo on the Provost at Ternhill.

We, Jimmy, Digger, and I, were now ready to be posted to our first Canberra squadron. We were given a choice of three postings: - Germany, Cyprus, or Singapore. They were all good and I really didn't mind which I went for but, having two older and more assertive crew members with me, they told me that I was volunteering for Singapore, "Aren't you?"

45 Sqn. Tengah

By late March 1961 we arrived at RAF Tengah in Singapore, having flown out on a chartered Britannia to Payar Lebar, the civil airport in Singapore at that time, with a cabin full of other serving members and their families.

We had stopped for refuelling at Istanbul and Bombay and even that was a terrific experience for me. These places were so *foreign*! This was well before mass international tourism and most travellers were either in the Services or on Government service.

I hadn't appreciated just how hot and humid Singapore was and had no concept of jetlag. I was a little confused as to why, for the first few days, I had been awake most of the night and wanted to sleep during the day.

Our first day consisted of walking around the station introducing ourselves to the Station Commander and various other senior officers to announce our arrival before ending up at 45 squadron, our home for the next two and a half years. We were wearing our new khaki tropical uniforms, bought in the UK to the correct service specification, only to find that everybody else was wearing tropical uniforms made locally in the Chinese tailor shops to their own specification. We stood out like sore thumbs; not only because of the uniforms but also because we were so white up against all the mahogany tans.

We were made very welcome on the Squadron, but I think I lowered the average age of the squadron members by several years as I had only just passed my 20th birthday the previous month. The rest of the guys seemed to be in their 30's and 40's. I had to pinch myself to appreciate where I was. I looked out of the crew room window to see a line of beautiful shiny silver Canberras with the squadron logo on the fin – a flying camel. I was now a squadron pilot!

We spent a few days settling in and being shown around Singapore in the evenings by some of the old hands on the squadron. Travel around the city was cheap because this was the age of pick-up taxis and pirate taxis. The pirates were unlicensed, private cars which cruised the streets looking for fares. They would stop to pick up anybody who looked as if they might want a cab. The pick-up taxis would cruise the main routes between villages and into the city, but they would be selling a seat and would stop for anybody until they were full. They were unbelievably cheap but completely unregulated – buyer beware!

We explored the open-air food markets which sold very exotic looking food for just a few dollars and I soon realised that we had made a good choice of posting. The exchange rate was very favourable – eight dollars to the pound – which made my monthly pay of around £50 go quite a long way. One of the first visits was to the local Chinese tailor who fitted us out with complete sets of tropical khaki uniforms which meant that, once we had spent some time in the sun, we could blend in with the rest of the squadron.

I quickly realised that I would need my own transport to get around the island. Whilst the taxis were plentiful on all the main routes, RAF Tengah was, like most RAF stations, out in the sticks and so off the regular bus and cruising taxi routes. I could not afford a car, however modest, at this time so I stretched my finances and bought a new Lambretta scooter. This was great until it rained, and it could really rain in Singapore. Turning up for a date looking like a drowned rat did not go down well so I would have to keep my eyes open for a car I could afford, but this would not be anytime soon.

There was a world of difference between life on our new squadron and our previous training stations. We had been accepted as adult and valuable members of the community and, after our first few check trips with the Squadron Training Pilot, we would become fully operational and could be called upon to do anything and everything that the other crews would do.

Most of the flying was around three hours of navigation at high level to the north of Singapore over the Malayan jungles and mountain ranges followed by bombing on our ranges in the South China sea or the Malacca Straits. We would sometimes allow ourselves to be high level 'targets' for the Australian fighter squadrons based in Butterworth, north western Malaya, who were flying American Sabres.

The only thing different from operating in the UK was that in this part of the world the thunderstorms were violent and could be dangerous. We had no weather radar and so, at night, it could be difficult to avoid flying into a very turbulent cloud which could be quite alarming. Over the years there had been accidents caused by flight into this extreme weather and so it was to be treated with the utmost respect. You only had to fly into the top of one of these storms once and experience the violent turbulence and probable lightning strikes to vow never knowingly to do it again.

Because of the heat and humidity of Singapore throughout the year our flying suits were designed accordingly. The outer suit was of a semi porous cotton material and we were supplied with air ventilated suits to wear underneath the outer flying suit. This AV suit was made of a thin nylon type material which incorporated numerous air tubes which could blow cooling air all over the body when connected to a special valve in the aircraft. In theory it sounds great, however in practice it was uncomfortable. Before climbing into the aeroplane, the nylon suit against the bare body made you sweat profusely and, even when you were taxying the aircraft on the ground before take-off, the cooling system seemed to be providing warm air. The net result was that most crews ditched the AV suit and just wore the flying suit over underwear. In Europe crews wore leather flying boots but in Singapore we wore specially designed canvas calf length lace-up boots with rubber soles and a full integral tongue which were ideal for walking through the jungle (should it become necessary).

In the 60's most of Malaya was covered in dense secondary jungle with the occasional town or village scattered throughout the peninsula. If an aircraft came down into this sort of terrain it was difficult for rescue teams to find it. We experienced this during my time in Singapore.

Of the several squadrons at RAF Tengah there was a Royal New Zealand Air Force squadron also flying Canberra B2's. On this particular stormy night one RNZAF aeroplane failed to make an expected position report and was never heard of again.

Obviously, this aircraft had crashed somewhere between his last position report and the next, missing report. This meant that the crash site could have been anywhere from Singapore to 100 miles north in the lower part of the Malayan peninsula: an exceptionally large area.

Air Sea rescue aircraft were launched from RAF Changi where they were based to fly over as much of this area as possible, looking for anything, possibly fire, which might give clues as to the crash site. As it was still dark and we were in the middle of the monsoon season, they were not very hopeful. The real search would start at first light and continue for as long as it took, day and night. For the next three days the whole of southern Malaya was flown over both at high and low level using as many pairs of eyes as possible. There was a Jungle rescue team standing by should anything be found.

On the third day a high-level Photo Reconnaissance Canberra from our PR squadron at Tengah saw something on a photo which *could* have been a small piece of aircraft. The Jungle Survival team were dropped by helicopter into the nearest accessible piece of jungle from the sighting and started to cut their way through to the site. In dense jungle like this, visibility was only a few feet and progress was slow.

When the rescue team reached the site, they identified pieces of aircraft wreckage as part of a Canberra and, sadly, the navigator's body still strapped into his ejector seat. There was no sign of the pilot or his seat.

At about this time, a very exhausted and bruised pilot from the crashed Canberra walked out of the jungle into a rubber plantation where he collapsed at the base of a rubber tree, knowing that the workers on a rubber plantation always collected the rubber dripping from the trees daily. He was picked up and taken to the nearest police station. The pilot, although badly bruised and shaken, was unharmed.

The jungle rescue team did, eventually, come across the pilot's parachute in the top of a tree, some way from the main wreckage and could see that he must have fallen about 60 feet to the jungle floor. With the branches below him having broken his fall and his having landed flat on his back in soft undergrowth, he was lucky not to have suffered serious injury or even death.

At the subsequent enquiry, the pilot stated that they had entered the top of a storm cloud which was so violent that he had lost control. In the rapid descent he was completely disorientated and shouted for the navigator to eject. On hearing what he thought was the explosion from the navigator's ejection he, himself, ejected.

He found himself in his parachute descending in the dark in a heavy rainstorm occasionally lit up with flashes of lightning. He could see that he was going to land in the upper branches of a tree and eventually found himself hanging from a branch with the ground somewhere, unseen, beneath him.

He was so uncomfortable in his tight webbing straps and, finding that he was unable to undo the buckles on his harness, cut his straps with the dinghy knife which every pilot has attached to his flying suit.

He fell from a great height, the branches breaking his fall somewhat, until he landed flat on his back in the undergrowth. He lay there, confused, and winded for a considerable time. When he felt able, he called out for his navigator. There was, of course, no answer.

Over the next three days he made his way in a northerly direction which, by chance, was the best he could have picked. It would bring him to the closest area of civilisation: any other direction would have been through miles and miles of virtually impenetrable jungle.

For the first couple of days the rain was almost continuous, and he spent the nights, wet and cold, curled up under whatever shelter the jungle could offer. By the third night thoughts of the Jungle Survival Course, that all crews had to attend, started to kick in. He stopped in the afternoon to gather branches and to build a shelter covered in leaves with a soft undergrowth bed to be ready for a more comfortable night.

He had found a couple of streams; water was generally not a problem in the jungle, and he had used his small pack of high energy rations which aircrew carried in a flying suit pocket. That night was dry, and he could see the clear, starlit sky through the overhead canopy, so he hadn't needed to build a waterproof shelter after all. The following day he made it out of the jungle.

Fortunately, accidents like this were rare, but it had been appreciated years before that the possibility of crew members finding themselves in jungle following a crash landing or ejection was very real.

Most of our operations were over Malaya which, at that time, was mainly uninhabited jungle. For this reason, the Jungle Survival School came into being at RAF Changi and all flying crews posted to Singapore or Malaya were required to attend.

It would last two weeks, the first of which was spent at the school at RAF Changi where you learned anything and everything about surviving in the jungle – What to eat and drink, how to build a shelter, etc. You even learned how to kill and cook a chicken by making an oven in the sand! It was never explained where you might find a chicken in the jungle but, by and large, it was all useful stuff.

The second week was spent in the jungle itself, near Mersing, a small town on the east coast of Malaya. During that week you were to put into practice all you had learned in the first week.

You can imagine, never having been in a jungle before, that you will be surrounded by wild and dangerous animals swinging from the trees and deadly poisonous snakes. Whilst, of course, there are animals in the jungle, some of them dangerous or poisonous, the chances of your meeting them are slight. The reason being that you are making so much noise crashing through the thick undergrowth that any self-respecting animal would have moved out of your way long before you reached it.

In our week in the jungle we did see one poisonous snake asleep in a shaft of sunlight on the ground which we walked around so he could continue his snooze. I think we also saw a bat, or maybe it was a flying fox.

By far the most unpleasant thing we had to cope with was the dreaded leach. They seemed to be everywhere, and they would, somehow, find their way through your clothing or your jungle boots to latch on to your flesh and do their thing.

Before turning in each night, we would strip off and inspect each other all over for the little (or not so little!) fat black bodies full of your blood on which they had gorged themselves during the day. You learned not to just pull them off as they could leave part of themselves buried in your body which could turn septic. Instead, you could either put a drop of iodine on them which made them feel unwelcome or, if you had a cigarette to hand, persuade them to leave by burning their bums. This seemed to be one of the advantages of smoking which is never mentioned!

At the end of the week in the jungle you would be transported back to the west coast of Singapore, still in a week-old smelly flying suit and, unwashed, would be released into the wild to make your own way back to the Jungle Survival School on the other side of the island. This was an 'escape and evasion' exercise.

You now had to evade the police and army who were out looking for you whilst you tried to arrive back at Changi without being caught. The penalty for being caught was 'torture' and interrogation by professional service interrogators until you 'broke' and were released for a much-needed shower, a meal and bed.

It was actually quite realistic, and the interrogation could be frightening, even if you knew they were not *actually,* going to harm you. All practice in what could occur during war. The course at Changi was so highly thought of that they even had US Airforce crews attending from their bases in the Pacific region. They were looking ahead to Vietnam.

AUSSIE EXERCISES

Most of our bomb dropping from Singapore was done with 8lb practice bombs. They would give us the necessary practice on dropping the real thing. However, it was necessary for us to experience dropping the sort of bomb we might have expected to drop in a war situation. This would be the 1000lb high explosive bomb, of which we could carry several.

Unfortunately, the sort of place where we might drop a bomb of this size were few and far between. One of the places was a range out in the Nicobar Islands in the Indian Ocean some way to the north west of Malaya. A navigation exercise would be planned to end up over Car Nicobar to drop our bomb.

I can remember when we dropped our first thousand pounder. Digger, in the nose, instead of shouting,

"Bomb Falling" shouted, "Christ, that's big!"

The effect on the aircraft was also quite marked. Having divested itself instantly of 1000lbs of weight we could feel the aircraft rise several feet. The other place where we had the opportunity of dropping a thousand pounder was on an island just off the coast of Australia some distance from Darwin. This would probably happen only once during our tour of duty in

Singapore and would invariably be as a joint exercise with the Royal Australian Airforce, who also flew Canberras.

We would fly our 'planes down to Darwin where we would meet up with the Aussie squadrons whose home base was in Brisbane and spend a couple of days around the Darwin area with them on joint exercises culminating in the dropping of our big bombs.

On the night of this exercise the briefing was given by the senior RAAF officer as it was their show.

All of the Canberras would take off at 2-minute intervals and would each fly different routes to end up at a specified time for each aeroplane to be over the target island to drop its 1000lb bomb. As the exercise was to be at night the target would be lit by flares.

Seemed straightforward enough to me. Jimmy, my navigator, would get us over the target on time and Digger, my bomb aimer, would release the bomb and all I had to do was fly the aeroplane. Simples!

Or maybe not...! The first I knew there was a problem was when Digger said,

"What colour are these flares supposed to be, because I can see several fires in front of me?" Silence from Jimmy and me until Digger said,

"OK, I'm pretty sure I have it…. Steady..Steady.. bomb gone, bomb falling, bomb doors closed!"

"Now let's get out of here", I said, "Before we find we out we've dropped 1000lbs of high explosive on some poor Aborigine sitting by his campfire".

No mention was made of collateral damage in the debriefing so I can only assume the bombing went to plan. A couple of the crews did mention some confusion due to spurious fires on the ground but, hey, this is war! The fires could well have been from previous bombs close to the target dropped by earlier Canberras.

We spent a further couple of days in Darwin which, in 1962, was a bit of a one-horse town. However, it did have a very respectable Swan Brewery and we contacted them to arrange a tour.

Several crews, both Aussies and Brits, turned up at the brewery in a coach and were made to feel very welcome. In the reception area there was a large stainless-steel wall in front of us with a tap in it which dispensed Swan Larger. We were told to pick up a glass from the table and to help ourselves! As they say, "A nod is as good as a wink," and for the next half an hour or so we spent a very pleasant 'reception'. Then came the tour of the facility which, I am certain, must have been interesting but nobody would ever remember.

Back at Tengah I think we all agreed that this had been a particularly good few days with our Australian counterparts and wondered if we could do it again sometime soon.

During 1961 it had been decided by the powers-that-be that the night fighter squadron based at Tengah and flying the now fairly old Meteor NF14's would have to update their squadron with the newer Javelin all-weather fighter. The one thing we did know about FEAF (the 'Far East Air Force' of the RAF) was that we featured quite low on the list for the provision of new equipment. Naturally, the Cold-War scenario demanded that the newest, more effective aeroplanes would be stationed in and around Europe and, what was left over, could safely be sent to Singapore. These delta winged Javelins were probably, at best, re-conditioned aeroplanes from other squadrons but they were certainly a step up from the Meteor.

They would be sent in groups of, perhaps, half a dozen or so aeroplanes from the UK out to Singapore. However, because of their very restricted range, they would be making quite a few refuelling stops on the way out. For each leg they would need accurate weather reports for the route in front of them because they wouldn't have the range to divert to any other airfield which could handle them. All-weather fighters, huh! This is where 45 Sqn and their Canberras came in.

A Canberra would fly to Delhi in India and meet them there on their flight out from the UK via their numerous refuelling stops. The plan was that we would then take off half an hour or so in front of them and land in Calcutta, all the while passing actual weather conditions to the Javelins behind us.

On the next sector, Calcutta to Rangoon in Burma, we would provide the same service. Finally, Rangoon to Bangkok, in Thailand before then flying down to Tengah. All very straightforward with the weather behaving itself all the way.

This, of course, could not take into account the one javelin which had a catastrophic engine failure over the river delta area in, what is now Bangladesh, but was then East Pakistan.

Both the navigator and the pilot had to eject over this jungle-cum-swampy area. The navigator was never found but the pilot was picked up some days later from the banks of the river by a Catalina flying boat. The pilot flying the Catalina performed a spectacular feat of flying by landing in a narrow stretch of the river, bounded on both sides by tall trees.

The rest of the ferrying went without incident and eventually 60 squadron ended up with a full complement of Javelins.

At Tengah we were, on a couple of occasions, visited by a flight of B57's from the US Air Force, based in Okinawa.

Their B57's were Canberras built under licence in the US and extensively modified for their own operations. We spent a week or so in joint exercises around Singapore and Malaya and later in the year we would get to return the favour by flying up to Okinawa to spend time with the B57 Squadron at their home base. It really was a different world on a USAF base. We were definitely the poor relations.

On our arrival an official welcoming dinner was provided for us at the Officers' Club. As well as our host USAF Squadron crews there were crews from other squadrons on the base. The meal was superb, much better than we were used to, but during the latter part of the evening a local Japanese dance band who had been playing in the background, suddenly struck up with a military sounding tune which prompted all of the USAF members of one of the squadrons to leap to their feet, stand to attention with hand over heart, to acknowledge what was obviously their squadron signature tune. This was repeated throughout the meal until all the USAF squadrons had been so honoured.

The stiff upper lip of the Brits quivered when our worst fears were realised as we were asked for our squadron tune for the band to play. We, of course, didn't have one but one of our pilots was dispatched to the stage to hum in the bandmaster's ear the only tune we could come up with – the RAF Marchpast! There followed what could have passed for a very successful TV comedy sketch with our pilot humming, tunelessly, the song punctuated by the Japanese bandmaster nodding furiously with numerous, "Ah, so's". The worst was yet to come when the bandmaster then hummed his rendition to his band followed by their playing a completely unrecognisable tune to which we, 45 sqn, were expected to leap to our feet, stand to attention, and tearfully hold our hands over our hearts. The Americans were bemused, and we were embarrassed, but it was all taken in good part with more exchanges planned for the future.

It seems that sometimes it is easier to understand your enemies than your allies!

One of our Air Traffic Controllers at Tengah was a guy called Max, and although he was about 15 years older than me, we shared an interest in cine photography and became quite friendly.

Max approached me one day and asked me, as he was going away for a couple of weeks, if I wouldn't mind running his car's engine every few days as the battery was suspect and would be totally dead if he left it unattended. It was kept in one of the asbestos open fronted garages at the bottom of a steep hill from the mess.

I readily agreed and put his car keys in my room and promptly forgot about them.

By now I had managed to acquire an elderly and rather beat-up car of my own, a Singer Sports model, as I had become a little disillusioned with riding around on my Lambretta in monsoon conditions. Consequently, I was spending the bulk of my off-duty time driving around Singapore, the last thing on my mind being Max's car.

Some two weeks later I was in the bar in the mess when I suddenly remembered that Max was due back the next morning and I hadn't run his engine, not even once!

I dashed down to the garage hoping against hope that I could get the car started. Not a chance! Dead as a Dodo. As the garages were at the bottom of the hill, I couldn't even push the car out to try to bump-start it. I could, I reasoned, tow his car out of the garage with my car and pull it up the hill towards the mess, stop my car on the handbrake, get out and go back to Max's car and put on his handbrake. I could then disconnect the towrope, get into Max's car and allow it to roll back towards the garages and try to bump-start it. Good plan! I could then run the engine to charge up the battery and Max would never know how unreliable a friend I had been.

The plan worked until I had pulled his car about twenty yards up the hill when, with a twang, my towrope broke and, in my rear-view mirror, I saw Max's car trundling down the hill, picking up speed and heading, straight as an arrow towards his garage.

Snatching at my handbrake, I leaped out of my car and ran down the hill in a desperate attempt to leap into the runaway vehicle to try to stop the inevitable crash. I didn't get within ten feet of my target, but fate was on my side as the car missed the sides of the garage and tracked accurately back into its space at about 10mph. The trouble was that there was nothing to stop it smashing through the asbestos back wall of the building before graunching to a stop, leaving a perfect hole in the wall the shape of Max's car!

I sheepishly returned to the mess where I managed to rope in a couple of drinkers from the bar to help me pull the car back through the hole in the garage and outside where I could get them to push start me. I was amazed to see that there was no sign of damage to the car but the hole in the garage said it all. Why I hadn't solicited help in the first place I will never know.

Having run Max's car to put some life back in the battery I decided that the best course of action was to leave it parked outside the mess and break the story slowly to Max when he returned. The last thing I wanted him to do was to go down to his garage where there would be no car but just a hole in the wall where his car should have been. I could tell him that I had put his car just outside the mess for his convenience and then take my time explaining how I had slipped on the mud whilst pushing his car out, lost control and watched, in horror, as it ran back into the garage and through the rear wall. Max was gentlemanly enough to accept my explanation and even thanked me for trying. Now, as long as he didn't talk to the guys who helped me push it out, I'd be safe!

NZ Lone Ranger

From time to time we had the opportunity to leave Singapore for the occasional few days in Hong Kong. This provided us with experience of flying away from base but was also seen as a 'jolly' and an opportunity to spend some time shopping in Kowloon.

The approach to the runway in Kowloon at Kai Tak was legendary and quite a test of flying skill. I would get to return there years later as a civil airline pilot to see the difference between landing a Canberra and a 747 Jumbo on this challenging strip of concrete.

During a tour on the Squadron each crew were tasked to take an aircraft on a solo mission to New Zealand. These were called 'Lone Rangers' and gave each of us the chance to experience operation away from base in a foreign environment with all the planning that such a trip entailed. Generally, on a standard tour of 2 ½ years you would expect a couple of trips to Hong Kong and one to New Zealand.

In June 1962 I was scheduled for my New Zealand Lone Ranger. My usual crew of two navigators were not available and so I had to team up with another couple from the squadron. I had flown with each of them before but didn't know them well operationally.

The plan was to depart from Tengah southbound over Indonesia, crossing the Java Sea and landing at Darwin in Australia's Northern Territories where we would stop at the RAAF base for the night. Because our early mark of Canberra, the B2, didn't have the long-range HF radio fitted we had to fly the route in company with an aircraft which was able to relay our regular position reports to the appropriate air traffic authority. We would be able to pass our reports to him by our shorter range VHF radio, so if we were within 100 miles of him this would be sufficient.

On this occasion there were two RAAF Canberras of a newer version fitted with HF radios who were flying from the Australian base in Butterworth, Malaya, down to Darwin and then on to Brisbane which would also be our next port of call. They agreed to land at Tengah on their way south to meet our crew and discuss our requirements.

The lead RAAF Canberra was being flown by their Squadron Commander, a wing commander, with a senior squadron leader navigator. The second RAAF aircraft was flown by a junior crew, a couple of flying officers like ourselves.

It was clear from the outset that we were a great inconvenience to the wing commander, and he made it quite plain that he would rather the RAF had made other arrangements. However, after the required briefing we took off and departed on our journey. We left Tengah bout ten minutes behind the two Aussies.

Climbing to our cruise altitude of around 40,000 feet we were able to pass our initial position reports on our VHF radios to Singapore without asking for Australian help. However, after an hour or so we noticed that our radio was beginning to crackle and we had great difficulty in passing our next report to the Aussies. We continued, transmitting 'blind' at each report point, that is, passing our report without receiving any acknowledgement in the hope that our transmitter was good but our receiver faulty. Sometimes we had an acknowledgement from the lead Canberras, sometimes not. Finally, after about four hours of flying, we were in range of Darwin with about a hundred miles to go. With a certain amount of difficulty, we were able to talk to the tower and proceeded with a normal landing.

As we sat on the tarmac at Darwin and shut our engines down our 'friendly' wing commander strode over to us and demanded that we got our 'bloody radio' fixed before leaving for Brisbane in the morning. Fortunately, the ground crews at the base were sympathetic to our plight and worked to fix our problem whilst we went to the mess for the night.

Before leaving the next morning the groundcrew chief told me that our radio had been in a 'hell of a mess' and showed signs of severe overheating. However, he told us that he had fixed the problem and we should be 'right'. With that reassurance we climbed aboard, started up and taxied out to the end of the runway.

Whilst I could talk to the tower and the other aircraft, I was vaguely uneasy that the reception was still pretty awful on a radio that would normally be crystal clear. I was not about to tell our Australian friends of my concerns so off we went in a stream take-off a few minutes after the leaders.

The route to Brisbane was pretty much direct, south of the Gulf of Carpentaria, passing close to Cloncurry and into Queensland. From leaving Darwin until arriving at Brisbane we didn't expect to see much as Australia is fairly empty and unfriendly in that part of the world.

We climbed up towards our cruising altitude and we could see the contrails of the two aeroplanes in front of us. We initially levelled off at around 40,000 feet and then set the controls to cruise climb to our maximum altitude of 48,000 feet. This was the most fuel-efficient way to operate – set the engines at maximum efficiency and allow the aeroplane to find its own altitude which would result in a gentle climb to our maximum height. 48,000 feet was the limit of our oxygen equipment and pressurisation even though the Canberra would climb higher than this.

Things were largely uneventful until we needed to have our first position report relayed after going out of the range of our VHF. This then became an action replay of yesterday with no contact to the Aussie aircraft. This time I was not quite as concerned as before as we were over friendly territory, could see the lead aircraft in the distance and the weather was pretty much perfect.

We were about halfway, around Cloncurry, when there was a muffled bang and we started to lose pressurisation. I noticed that our cockpit altimeter, which normally showed an internal altitude of 25,000 feet, was beginning to 'climb'. This meant that at 48,000 feet, if we ended up unpressurised, even breathing the pure oxygen through our masks would be insufficient to stop us becoming anoxic. We had to descend to remain conscious, but if we descended, we would use more fuel and would have insufficient to get to Brisbane, or indeed, back to Darwin. Conundrum!

For some obscure reason I suddenly remembered a conversation I had overheard in the bar back at base some weeks before. It seemed that this pilot had experienced a pressurisation failure which had been preceded by radio problems. At the time he had not connected the two, but it subsequently turned out that the hot air for the pressurisation had a supply pipe that passed through the lower equipment hatch where the radio happened to live. The final fracture in this pipe had blasted super-heated air over the radio with obvious results! Prior to the final fracture the pipe had a split in it which had caused the overheating of the radio. Eureka! He had then been told that pressurisation could be partly returned by opening the pipes to the air ventilated suits and allowing it to discharge into the cockpit. We wore these suits, of the type that you see astronauts wearing, and had them connected to this cool air supply.

'OK guys, disconnect your suits from the supply pipe and turn on the flow to max'.

It started to work! Slowly the cockpit altitude descended but it was freezing in that cabin! The air for the suits was, naturally, cool and the outside temperature at that altitude was approaching -56 centigrade! but we didn't have to descend, just yet anyway.

We managed to keep the leading Canberras in sight and, in fact, slowly closed the gap between us.

I was aware that flying into a busy airspace with no radio would not be the best of ideas. It seemed to me that if we tagged on to the leader in loose formation, we could follow him around to a landing confident that he would have realised what we were doing and Air Traffic would be in the loop.

Apart from the silence in our headsets the approach and landing at Brisbane was uneventful. It was a blessed relief to descend to the warmer, lower atmosphere.

On the ground the wing commander had obviously decided that he wouldn't waste his time by entering into any conversation with us. Fine by me! In fact, as this was his final destination, he had washed his hands of us entirely.

After a night stop here the plan was that we, and the junior Aussie crew, would depart for New Zealand the next morning, but first I had to see to our sick aeroplane.

I told the groundcrew chief of my suspicions about the hot air supply in the lower bay and he was amazed that it was exactly as I had suggested. This gnarled old professional seemed to have a new respect for a young 21-year-old RAF pilot and agreed to pull out all the stops to repair us by the next morning.

The morning was bright and clear, we had a working aeroplane (at last) and we had rid ourselves of the wing commander. The two young flying officers who would now accompany us down to NZ even chatted to us in a half friendly fashion.

The departure from Brisbane went without a hitch and we climbed up into a clear blue winter's sky whilst we set course across the Tasman Sea for New Zealand. We had decided to fly in loose formation separated by a couple of hundred yards or so, just to be on the safe side. Our pressurisation and radios worked well, and the flight was quite pleasant with a totally uneventful approach and landing into the RNZAF base of Ohakea, at the southern end of the North Island.

We taxied in, parked as directed by the ground crew, shut the engines down and climbed out looking forward to a very pleasant couple of days in NZ. This was not to be!

We were met on the tarmac by the Station Duty Officer who told us that the mess had an official dinner that evening, accommodation would be difficult and, as we obviously didn't have our formal 'mess kits' with us we would be excluded. In fact, he obviously thought, but didn't say, 'You're going to have a miserable time so why don't you go somewhere else?' He did, however, suggest that we could fly up to the RNZAF base at Auckland, Whenuapai, where we would be assured of a friendly welcome.

We didn't take much persuading, especially when he told us that the weather up country would be much as it was there, if not, better. It was a straightforward route up the west coast, and we could make it comfortably without refuelling fully and just have our main tanks topped up. The SDO even offered to file our flight plan for us (nice man) to save us time. We could almost hear his sigh of relief as he waved us off.

It was now late afternoon locally and mid-winter in NZ and we were soon on our way north. Again, we were in loose formation and feeling rather satisfied with a decision well made.

The scenery was spectacular, and we passed Mount Ruapehu on our right and saw snow blowing across the top of the mountain. It was a scene from a postcard. We were at about 10,000 feet and there was broken cloud above us with a darkening blue sky in between. The further north we flew the thicker the cloud became and the lower the cloud base. In fact, we either had to descend to keep below it or fly into it.

By now we were in radio contact with Auckland, en-route to RNZAF base at Whenuapai. We heard them passing a weather report to another aircraft – '200 ft cloud base, visibility ¼ mile in heavy rain'. Where the hell had *that* come from? I was now severely regretting not having picked up a weather forecast for our route. I was still in formation with the Aussie aircraft and this was now *close* formation.

We had been directed by air traffic control to descend into a holding pattern due to other traffic and we were in that heavy rain – in the dark! I had never flown the Canberra (a fairly sizeable aeroplane) in formation as close as this; certainly not in rain; certainly not in the dark and in cloud! I was sweating buckets and working as I had never done before. I could see the wing tip and nav light of our no. 1 and vaguely make out his fuselage outline.

I asked our nav to check the approach charts for Whenuapai in case we had to break off from the leader and make our own way in for a landing. I was shocked when he told me that he had no paperwork for this part of New Zealand as we hadn't expected to come here! This is when, as captain of the aircraft, I realised just where the buck stops. I was now committed to remaining in close formation for the duration.

We were directed by ATC to enter the standard twin locator holding pattern as published on the charts which we didn't have, which both aeroplanes had difficulty with. It seemed that the pattern had been designed for much slower prop aeroplanes and a couple of jets, in formation, tearing around in cloud in the dark, were upsetting things somewhat. For this reason, they picked us out of the holding pattern fairly early and brought us round under radar for a radar-controlled approach to the runway.

Meanwhile I continued to slavishly stick to my no. 1 and took my clues from him as he lowered his flaps and then his gear. We continued down and at about 200 feet the very blurred, wet lights of the runway appeared ahead.

No. 1 was cleared to land, and the radar controller directed us, no. 2, to climb straight ahead and enter the holding pattern for a further approach.

'Oh, no way', I was in sight of the runway and declared that I was executing a tight, low level circuit to the left, and would come round for a visual landing. He cleared me to the tower frequency, and I got my landing clearance as I came round just below the cloud base and lined up for a landing. The runway was wet, *very* wet, and in lashing rain it was like landing on the surface of a puddle. After touchdown, I applied full brakes and, with a certain amount of snaking, slowed the aircraft for the final turn off the runway at the end. Phew! I don't think I have been so pleased to get on the ground in all my life.

An inspection of my tyres when we climbed out showed a certain amount of bubbling on the rubber, a typical sign of aquaplaning. I didn't really have time to think much about this as the two Aussie flying officers came bounding across the tarmac towards us to pour praise upon us for 'spectacular' formation flying. If only they knew!

Two days later the trip back to Singapore was boring almost with nothing going wrong but we had made a couple of Australian friends!

During this trip I had learned that the captain of the aircraft is responsible for almost everything and, as such, he takes nobody's word for anything without double checking.

B15'S

During 1962 45 Sqn began to re-equip with a newer, more powerful, and versatile Canberra. This would be the B15, which in fact was a re-incarnated and refurbished (so what's new?) version of the B6.

In order to get our hands on these aeroplanes the Squadron would fly our old B2's back to the UK, one crew at a time, and, after a few days flight testing our replacement aeroplanes in the UK, would fly the B15 back out to Singapore.

My crew's turn came on 15th October when we took our ageing B2 from Tengah to Wroughton in the UK via Rangoon, Calcutta, Karachi, Teheran, Akrotiri, Luqa and Lynham.

We arrived there just in time to see the confrontation between the USA and the USSR over missiles based in Cuba come to a head. We were put on a standby footing as a trained RAF crew in case war broke out. Fortunately, we were spared and now this serious ramping up of Cold War tensions would be remembered as the 'Cuban Missile Crisis', the nearest the world came to nuclear war.

We were now released from our standby and, after the 'shakedown' testing of our B15, we prepared to return to Singapore. This went quite smoothly, and we were able to miss out landing at Luqa in Malta due to the extra range of the B15. We arrived back in Singapore exactly three weeks after leaving there.

Over the next few weeks there followed a comprehensive 'conversion' on to this new aeroplane and other crews continued to fly to UK to replace the remaining B2's with B15's. By the end of 1962 there were no B2's left on the squadron.

In December of 1962 there were rumours of trouble from guerrilla groups in Borneo attacking settlements in Sarawak. Borneo was a divided island, the southern half of which was held by Indonesia and the northern half by Sarawak, Labuan, Brunei, and Sabah. The Indonesians were concerned that these northern states might be incorporated into the newly proposed Malaysian state. The Indonesians did not want this to happen and so it was that trouble started brewing and it could be assumed that the guerrillas were being supplied by Indonesia.

This all came to a head on 8th December 1962 when a senior British Foreign Office representative needed to fly out to Kuching in Sarawak for urgent talks with the local governing body. A Canberra from 45 Sqn would take him there and I was nominated for the job. It was a Saturday and normally we would have the afternoon off duty, but I was told to prepare to fly this gentleman across to Labuan, a small island bordering Sarawak.

As we sat, uncomfortably, on that Saturday afternoon in our Canberra in the heat and humidity outside 45 Squadron, we waited for our VIP passenger to arrive.

After fifteen minutes or so a black government limousine drew up alongside the aircraft and the driver opened the rear door for a tall, sophisticated gentleman to emerge. He was straight out of 'Yes, Minister.' He had the Foreign Office uniform of a dark pinstripe suit, a briefcase but no furled brolly (he must have left it in the car).

Whilst we watched, the groundcrew helped him into a flying suit, over the top of his pinstripe suit! Goodness knows how he was feeling, struggling there in the direct tropical sunshine. We were hot and sweaty with just underpants under our flying suits! Next, to add insult to injury, he was strapped into a parachute and then made to put on a cloth flying helmet. All in all, he looked like a trussed-up chicken; cooked, of course!

After this little show was over, he was helped into the aircraft and strapped into the small fold-down seat next to me and plugged into the radio distribution box for that seat. The door was now closed, and we were ready to start our engines. I asked our passenger on the intercom if he was ready. Looking as though he had just escaped from being trapped under a sunlamp for an hour, a sweaty, red face just grinned at me but said nothing. I took that as a 'yes' and so we started our engines and taxied out to the runway.

All the way out I tried to engage our F.O. man in conversation with no success. I realised there must be a problem with his radio distribution box. These boxes give you the facility of listening to any of the radio frequencies being received in the aircraft, including all the navigation aids. When I checked his box all the buttons for 'receive' were selected and he was listening to every conceivable frequency we had! I switched them all off, except for the intercom. He immediately said, "Thank God for that! I think I was listening to everyone in the world." He could now hear me alone on the intercom.

Once we were airborne, we started to cool down and our passenger even looked as though he was beginning to enjoy the ride. The weather was mainly clear, and we had a good view of the Islands en-route and, in the latter stages, the coastline of Borneo as we approached Labuan.

We dropped our man from the F.O. off without incident but the troubles in Borneo continued for a number of years and the Singapore Squadrons continued to be involved, mainly the helicopter Squadrons, dropping and picking up troops in the troubled areas of Sarawak and Sabah. This little war was known as 'Confrontation' and commonly called the Undeclared War.

ONE WHEEL?

Towards the end of January 1963, I had completed nearly 2 years on 45 Squadron. All our old B2's had gone, and we were totally equipped with the B15. The B15 brought with it more powerful engines, the Avon 109, better all-round equipment and a rocket delivery system which could deliver a large number of 2" rockets. For me, as a 21-year-old pilot with under 900 hrs flying experience, this was like having the key to the toy shop.

My crew and I had been authorised to fly a Navex (navigation exercise) over Malaya followed by a low-level bombing mission on our local range island of China Rock, just to the north east of Singapore in the South China Sea. For this part of the exercise, we were carrying several 8lb practice bombs in our bomb bay. The B15 had the same crew of three as the B2.

We departed south from Tengah in the west around the south of the island to Changi where I had decided to shoot a few circuits prior to departing for the Navex. This gave me the chance to visit the 'posh' end of Singapore and to show off the B15 to the transport guys based at Changi.

The first circuit was routine and the two navigators, Jimmy Milne and Bob Burr, had slipped into boredom mode whilst I enjoyed myself. However, after the 'roller' on the second circuit I was vaguely concerned that I was left with a red unlocked light on my main port gear after selecting undercarriage up. This was a fairly low-level concern but became more interesting when a recycling of the gear still left me with a red light.

Having decided that it could be a false indication from a faulty microswitch I requested a low, slow fly by the tower for a visual inspection. Through his binoculars, the controller said it looked as if the wheel was out of its locked position and seemed to be partially up.

There was nothing for it but to go home but first we needed to rid ourselves of the bombs. It did not seem wise to be carrying them in our belly if there was a possibility of having to land with no wheels, even if they were low yield bombs. Off to China Rock then and back to base after jettisoning them.

Tengah had been warned of our predicament and, after a further low pass inspection in front of the tower, an airborne Hunter from one of our fighter squadrons flew underneath us in formation for a closer inspection. No amount of looking was going to bring that wheel down and the situation appeared to be that the wheel was over the top of the undercarriage door which was being held in its closed position. We subsequently found out that it was a sequence valve malfunction – the wheel couldn't come down whilst the door was closed, and the door couldn't open because the wheel was holding it up!

Whatever we decided to do it would be much better not to be full of fuel if we were to skid along the runway on our belly. We were carrying wing tip tanks, each holding about 1900lbs of fuel, so we needed to be rid of those. Flying at about 1500ft, over the sea to the south of Tengah, I had the pleasure of being able to operate the yellow and black striped control which jettisoned the tanks. They left cleanly – one second they were there, the next gone!

That day, RAF Tengah was being visited by the Air Officer Commanding from HQ in Changi and so there was a gathering of senior officers in the tower all anxious to put in their two penn'orth of advice and experience in an attempt to avoid a disaster. In discussion with the tower, I told them that my preference was to lower what gear we had and land on the good wheel rather than landing totally wheels up.

I would have to hold the port wing up as long as possible, before lowering it gently to the ground as we lost lift. This was agreed but there was a suggestion that we performed a fast approach and landing 'bumping' the good wheel on the runway in an attempt to shake down the stuck one before our final landing. This actually achieved nothing but a great deal of glee from the gathering pilot community on the ground who thought they were about to witness a truly great spectacle of a Canberra landing 40 kts too fast, halfway up the runway, with no chance of stopping before the end.

"Good grief, he's lost it......this'll be good!"

Next, we had to lose fuel and prepare for a crash landing. We were now back in the realms of the emergency checklist – First, Jimmy had to jettison the navigators' hatch (our means of escape after a crash landing). We then had to replace the ejector seat safety pins in each of the three seats to make them 'safe' in the event of a very bumpy arrival, and finally, disconnect our parachute harnesses just leaving a tightly buckled seat harness in place. We wouldn't be needing parachutes on the ground and we needed as few restraints as possible in the event of a rapid exit.

Whilst we worked our way through the checklist, the fire services at Tengah were laying a carpet of foam down the left side of the runway from about halfway down to lessen the friction when our wing lowered to the ground.

I experienced a very alarming situation when the nav's blew their hatch. The explosive bolts blew it away cleanly but what I was not ready for was the sudden decrease of pressure in the cockpit which produced a thick fog, reducing the visibility to zero. The B15 had no auto pilot and at 1500ft, with no sight of the instruments or, indeed, anything else, I had a moment of quiet panic until, within seconds, the fog cleared as rapidly as it had appeared. Phew!

Having flown around reducing fuel we were now as ready as we were going to be for the landing. The powers that be in the tower informed me that records showed a Canberra landing on 1 main wheel would be able to 'keep its wing up until about 65kts when the wing would lose lift and touch the ground. The aircraft would then veer off in the direction of the low wing describing a path of about 100yds radius.' Exactly what I thought! Bearing this in mind, it had to be as smooth a landing as I could make it to the right side of the runway, short of the foam, so that the wing would be lowering as we slid into the foam strip.

The touchdown was smooth and felt surprisingly normal. I kept the nose high after touchdown to reduce speed and, sure enough, at around 65kts I was unable to prevent the port wing from dropping. I was ready for the expected veer off to the left and with full right rudder, applied differential braking to counter the swing. The swing didn't happen! In fact, if anything we started to slew off to the right and I had to lessen the brake on that side. All the while we were passing by, and missing by several feet, the foam to our left and as the aircraft came to rest, virtually in a straight line, it gave a little kink to the left.

The crash-landing drill now was to shut down the engines, kill the power, exit the aircraft out of the top through the hole where the navs' hatch had been, and jump to the ground.

The navigators left first, and I followed, scrambling onto the nearest nav's ejector seats to heave myself up.

I have a clear recollection of one of my feet catching in the seat blind handle which operates the ejector mechanism and the handle partially pulling out towards the firing point, but no fears, as the seat had been made safe by the insertion of the safety pin. It wasn't until after the seats had been checked by the armourer, the first into the cockpit, that it was discovered both safety pins were missing from the navigators' seats. I very nearly had a spectacular departure from the cockpit!

The subsequent enquiry found that in all probability the turbulent airflow in the navs' compartment after the hatch was blown was enough to pull on the large red safety warning discs attached to the pins and pull them out of the seats and away into the slipstream. The drill for future cases was amended to include the removal of the disc in these circumstances.

The other surprise was that our B15 had rocket pylons fitted under the wings which prevented the down-going wing tip touching the ground and had acted as a mini skid – hence the lack of a turn to the left. For this reason, the aircraft suffered minimal damage and was back in the air in a matter of days.

What did I learn? Well, nothing goes exactly according to plan but there is always something useful to be gleaned from every mishap which all adds to your data base of knowledge and may well be indispensable on some future occasion. It's called experience.

From time-to-time ejector seats would be updated by the British manufacturers, Martin Baker, who made seats, not only for the British services, but also for many foreign forces, including the USA. These seats had saved many lives but there were always limitations to their successful use.

Generally, the stricken aircraft had to be at a minimum height above the ground of 1,000 feet and flying, more or less, level. A steep dive would obviously compromise that 1,000 feet limitation. The next requirement was that the aircraft had to be travelling at a minimum speed of 90 knots, which would provide sufficient airflow to deploy the parachute effectively. Naturally, in an emergency, one could never guarantee satisfying all these limitations and so Martin Baker were continually working towards a seat which could operate from ground level and, preferably, at less than 90 knots.

One particular knotty problem was that the more powerful the explosive charge which fired the seat the more likely the occupant was to sustain compression fractures of the spine. The solution to this problem was still not available at this time but, eventually, would lead to the use of rocket charges which produced an increasing acceleration compared to the extremely high forces of an instant explosion.

Whilst I was at Tengah a new seat had been produced which could eject a pilot safely from ground level but still at 90 knots. It was decided that the flying community should watch a demonstration of the seat operating from the back of a truck being driven across the airfield at as great a speed as possible. This, it was hoped, would instil in us a sense of trust in our new equipment.

On the appointed day the assembled group of flying crews watched the impressive demonstration of the seat firing upwards, the dummy pilot separating from the seat and crashing to the ground, parachute unopened, and the seat landing with a thump dangerously close to the dummy. This brought a thunderous applause from the crowd. Whilst the truck hadn't reached 90 knots this demonstration did nothing to bolster our confidence so, back to the drawing board! We were now reaching the limit in the use of explosive charges in the seat but, however the demonstration had gone, we were better off with the new seat.

In the latter part of my tour at Tengah I had to sit my 'B' exams. This covered a variety of subjects mainly dealing with an Officers knowledge of RAF Law and administration and the responsibility of a senior officer in an RAF unit. Passing this exam was necessary before promotion from Flying Officer to Flight Lieutenant. With a pass of the 'B', promotion would be automatic after three and a half years as Flying Officer. I would qualify for this in August of 1964, about a year after leaving 45 Sqn in August of 1963.

Before leaving Tengah, I had to indicate my preference for my next posting. My choices were: - Apply to fly for a further tour on another Canberra Sqn., which would be either Germany or Cyprus; apply to fly, initially, as a co-pilot on the 'V' Force, our high level strategic nuclear strike force, or apply to become a flying instructor, either basic or advanced.

I felt that I should now move on from Canberras and, rumour had it, that a tour on the 'V' Force was quite unattractive due to the long hours on QRA (Quick Reaction Alert) as the primary strike force in a nuclear war. Also, after a tour as co-pilot, you would automatically be in line for a tour as captain, thereby committing you to five years flying a 'V' bomber. The MOD would automatically look to ex Canberra pilots, being bomber trained, to fly the 'V's.

The best way to avoid this was to volunteer for instruction! Hence, I applied to attend the Central Flying School at RAF Little Rissington to do the QFI (Qualified Flying Instructor) course. I rather fancied becoming an instructor on the Gnat, a small, fast advanced jet trainer. Maybe I would have my photo taken in front of the jet to go on the front of a recruiting pamphlet!

I was accepted for a course at CFS, and would start there in the late autumn of 1963, after a spot of leave at home in the UK.

221 COURSE, CFS

The thing about flying is that you never escape the clutches of frequent checks and training, and so I now found myself back as a student, or trainee. All the pilots on the CFS course were experienced aviators with, typically, in excess of 1000 hours flying but it was now made plain to us that we needed to learn to fly 'properly'.

"Over the past few years, you have, almost certainly, picked up a few undesirable habits and we need to iron those out of you," we were told. "After all, unless you can fly perfectly yourselves, how can you expect to teach others to fly to the standard required by the RAF?"

They had a point, I'm sure, and we were about to find out.

The course was to be split into two halves: for the first 50 hours or so we would fly the Piston Provost (yes, the aircraft on which I had done my initial training) under the supervision of a staff instructor who would make sure that when we said we were flying at 1000 feet, it was not 999 or 1001!

The flying was very demanding but very satisfying. At the end of this part of the course we would fly with a senior staff instructor on our FHT (Final Handling Test) where everything had to be pretty much perfect.

From there we would progress to the type of aircraft on which we would be instructing at a Flying Training School. The choice was: -

1) the Jet Provost, the new all-through jet trainer which replaced the Piston Provost and Vampire, to make a single aircraft type for initial and advanced training. New pilots joining the RAF now would only be trained on these jets with no propeller aircraft experience, from first flight to 'wings'.

2) the gnat fast jet for advanced weapon training, or

3) the Chipmunk initial propeller trainer for all University Air Squadrons. Each of the large Universities throughout the UK would have its dedicated squadron where university students could join to learn to fly with no obligation to join the RAF afterwards. The hope was that some of these cadets would join the RAF as pilots or, if they didn't, might find themselves in a future government or other high-powered positions where they might be 'air-minded' enough to help the RAF.

My first choice was the gnat, so, naturally, I was told I would be going to a UAS (University Air Squadron) to instruct University cadets on the Chipmunk!

I complained to our CO but was told that I should feel honoured as a UAS posting was bestowed upon us by the Ministry of Defence and should be seen as a career move. When the courses arrived at CFS, I was told, the MOD had already decided on which pilots would go to the UAS's and the rest would be selected at local level and posted to other types depending upon their performance on the course. I tried to feel honoured, but it came out as disappointment!

This meant that the second half of my course would now be on the Chipmunk where we would concentrate on the teaching aspect of flying.

The pattern would be that your instructor would brief you, as though you were a student with no flying experience, both on the blackboard before flight, and then to follow that lesson in the air.

For the next flight roles were swapped. You had to act as the instructor, giving a full blackboard briefing to your instructor, who was now the 'dumb' student, and then following that through with the exercise in the air. These instructors were masters at being *really* dumb and would try to wrong-foot you at every opportunity, a great way to make you aware of the possible pitfalls.

The course would work its way through from the very first 'Effect of Controls' exercise to advanced aerobatics and formation flying. Flying accurately was one thing but flying and talking at the same time to explain precisely what you were doing and what the student was to expect, was quite another. The first time your instructor said to you, "You know, you really taught me something that time," was a very satisfying feeling.

At the end of the course, you would become a QFI (Qualified Flying Instructor) and would be awarded a rating. Invariably, unless you were very special, this would be a B2 rating. Over time, on a squadron, this would progress to a B1 then A2 and finally, A1. After the appropriate checks, of course.

It was whilst I was on the CFS course that I met my future wife, Hilary. She was a young WRAF Pilot Officer; one of the first women Air Traffic Controllers in the Air Force and was working in the tower at Little Rissington. Being single, she was also living in the mess, which meant I didn't have far to walk her home.

My posting, as a fresh B2 QFI, was to be to White Waltham, which was the home of the London University Squadron.

I would start my tour in the Spring of 1964 and would be one of six instructors, all of whom were vastly more experienced than me. Our Flight Commander was an ex-wartime Spitfire pilot!

ULAS

W hite Waltham is close to Maidenhead, in Berkshire, and is home to many private 'club' aeroplanes. It is a grass airfield with no concrete runways, and the University of London Air Squadron (ULAS) occupied its own building away from the private aeroplane clubs. On the squadron we had half a dozen Chipmunks in which we would do all our instructional flying with the ULAS cadets. The flying was programmed to fit in with university life and so most of the flying was done at weekends with some fitting in between Wednesday and Friday. Monday and Tuesday would be our 'weekend'.

As soon as I arrived on the squadron, I was told that I was to accompany a rugby team of our cadets on a short tour of RAF stations in Germany where they would play against local teams. It would appear that the other instructors, all being married, had decided, before I had arrived on the squadron, that the new, unmarried, Flying Officer was the ideal person to be in charge of a group of hard-drinking, partying, university students, all of whom were around my age. This, even though I had never played rugby in my life (it wasn't on the curriculum at King Edward's School) and had no knowledge of the mysteries of the game. General Duties Officer, see?

Flying from White Waltham was interesting because we were underneath the outer reaches of the London control zone. This meant that, after take-off we had to remain low to keep beneath the base of the zone to avoid civil aircraft operating to and from Heathrow. We had to fly in a narrow corridor to the west after take-off until we passed Reading when we could climb, unrestricted, for our exercises.

This was now my first experience of instructing with proper students and so I could see for real whether I was teaching them anything.

As a B2 instructor I could bring the student up to the point of his first solo but couldn't actually send him off on his own. He would have to fly with an A rated QFI for a solo check. This could be quite frustrating because, to send a student off on his own, you needed to assess not only his ability to take-off and land safely, but also whether he had the confidence to perform on his own.

As a rough guide, you needed to see three consecutive, well flown circuits followed by three acceptable landings. It was possible, if you had any doubts, to go beyond that point where the student might lose confidence in himself and land badly which made him feel worse. To hand him over to somebody else, a different instructor, with a different manner, might bring him 'off the boil.' Once he had flown his first solo, he *knew* he could do it again and so he was on his way.

One of the major differences between flying UAS students and regular RAF students was that, on the Air Squadron, these cadets were only flying part time. You had no idea (but might fairly quickly find out) what their motivation was for joining the squadron. In some cases, it was because a friend had told them that you might as well go along for some free flying, and it's a good 'club' to belong to. I had first-hand experience of this attitude at the beginning of the new university intakes for that year.

It was part of our duty to go along to the college 'crushes' and set up an RAF 'stall' to attract and recruit new members of the college to our squadron. We were one of many stalls trying to attract prospective candidates and might find ourselves alongside some very dubious stalls who might only be seen once a year trying to relieve new students of a joining fee.

Naturally, we had to assure anybody who stopped to enquire that, no, they weren't signing on to join the RAF but, yes, there were certain commitments they had to make and, no, it wouldn't cost them anything, in fact they would pick up some small allowances to offset any expenses.

We would end up with a list of names, a good few of which could be discounted for various reasons, and then they would have to pass an interview and a medical before being accepted. This would be carried out at our Air Headquarters, a very respectable building in West Kensington, a stone's-throw from the V&A Museum.

In the basement of our HQ, we had a bar and kitchen/dining area for our regular town gatherings, generally once a month. This was always popular with the cadets where they could buy a decent steak meal and a beer for knockdown prices. They would have to cook the meal themselves but there was never a shortage of volunteers for the kitchen.

In the summer of 1964, I was promoted to Flight Lieutenant, having served three and a half years as Flying Officer, and Hilary and I got married and were awarded a married quarter at White Waltham.

This was unusual for two reasons. First was that, as I was under 25 years old, the RAF in their wisdom, would not recognise that you were 'old enough' to warrant any consideration regarding married accommodation or marriage allowance on your pay. They just ignored your marriage completely. The second reason was that White Waltham had so few officers on the station that they had a surplus of married quarters – so the boy might as well have one! They still collected rent. This ridiculous pay differential was corrected some years later when the pay of officers was based upon their rank and not their circumstances.

After 9.1 months of marriage, our first son, Andrew, was born, in May of 1965.

I didn't find instructing on the Air Squadron very fulfilling but, once a year, we got to have some fun when the students went home for their summer holidays.

We would be scheduled to run a course of air experience for emergency services, i.e., the Police Force and Fire Services. The reason being that, in the event of serious unrest or, possibly, nuclear war, it might be necessary for these gentlemen to fly with us in our little chipmunks around the country 'spotting' from the air over places which might be inaccessible to them from the ground. It was also an opportunity for us to have a joint knees-up in the mess or down at the local pub after flying. Having your own policemen in the group at the pub was really quite handy, as you could imagine! These gentlemen thoroughly enjoyed, not only the flying, but also the soirees, and were anxious to come again the following year.

Towards the end of 1965 I had been on the squadron for about 18 months and, under normal circumstances, would have had to serve a further year. However, I caught sight of a signal in the boss' office asking for volunteer QFI's to go out to the newly independent Zambia (which the year before had been Northern Rhodesia) and fly, on 'loan service' for the Zambia Air Force (ZAF).

Successful applicants would be employed as QFI's to train the first Zambian pilots. Another overseas posting seemed quite attractive, especially in a nice warm climate, and to clinch it, there would be loan service pay of twenty-two shillings and sixpence per day on top of the RAF salary!

I knew something about Zambia because my parents had recently gone out there to live whilst my stepfather, who had been in the British army for a large number of years, had joined the Zambian armed forces on a contract. I decided to phone the contact for the posting in the MOD to test the water, feeling that they had probably been inundated with applications from very much better qualified QFI's than myself. I have to say that I was a little alarmed when he immediately came back with,

"When can you go?"

"Uhm, I'm really only trying to find out about the posting, you know, how long, where is the base, how big is the training school, etc. etc?"

"Well, I can't tell you a great deal, but I believe you would be stationed in Livingstone, a lovely spot, right near the Victoria Falls, and the school is really just starting, and you would be instructing on Chipmunks, initially. Can you go at the end of the week?"

"Well, look, I need to speak to my wife who knows nothing about this as I've only just seen the signal. Even if I agree to go, I couldn't possibly leave until the end of the month."

"That will have to do, then. Can you give me a ring back tomorrow and we'll be able to tie everything up?"

I was a bit nonplussed. I hadn't mentioned this to Hilary, nor had I run it by my boss to see if he minded my leaving him and the rest of the squadron in the lurch and short-handed. I wouldn't miss White Waltham, per se, but the fact that the MOD was desperate enough to grab the first person who phoned in meant that the rest of the world probably knew something that I didn't. Didn't they always say in the services, "Never volunteer for anything."?

I was committed to phoning back the next day as he knew where I was and how to find me, so I had to satisfy myself on a few points. How would I travel out there? What would I need to take with me? Would I still be a full member of the RAF or am I transferring to a foreign air force? Can my wife and son travel out with me? How long is the tour? Is any sort of accommodation provided? Is there anybody there on this FTS whom I might know?

In the event, Hilary thought it would be a good idea and the boss wasn't nearly as upset as I thought he should have been! It looked as though I was committed to going out to deepest, darkest Africa by the end of the month. Because I would be three months short of the magical 25 years old Hilary and young Andrew would not be able to join me until then. They would not be flexible on that point.

"Oh, and there is another QFI out there whom you may know – Jock Byrne."

Yes, hallelujah, I did know Jock. He was one of our instructors on vampires at Oakington and a thoroughly nice guy. If it was good enough for Jock, it would probably be OK for me.

At the beginning of November 1965, I found myself boarding a BOAC VC10 at Heathrow on my way, alone, out to Lusaka, the capital of Zambia.

ZAMBIA AIR FORCE

O n arrival at Lusaka, Zambia, I was met by an RAF flight sergeant who gave me a tired sort of salute with,

"Flight Lieutenant Warren? Get your bags and follow me. We have a ZAF aircraft waiting to take you down to Livingstone."

The flight was a little over an hour and as we approached the airport, I could see the Zambesi river snaking away just beyond the town and the spray from the Victoria Falls forming its own cloud and looking spectacular.

Descending the aircraft steps, I saw a beaming Jock Byrne standing at the bottom. He stretched out his hand and said, predictably,

"Doctor Livingstone, I presume?"

"Jock, good to see you." I had thought of calling him 'Sir', because he had been one of my instructors, but, as we were both Flight Lieutenants, I felt I could get away with being familiar!

"I didn't get to find out much about the FTS in Livingstone from the MOD but how big a setup is this?"

"You and I are it, my old mate. The only QFI's in Zambia to my knowledge. We have two aeroplanes, chipmunks, one of which is in a flyable state and was given to the ZAF by the RAF and the other was picked up cheaply from a local Rhodesian farmer and needs a bit of work. I think he had been giving his pigs a ride in it. On the plus side we have a bit of time to get the school up and running because we don't have any students yet. Oh, and we don't have any training accommodation for the school, but I have managed to scrounge the flysheet of an eight-man tent, a few chairs and a blackboard to get us started."

"Good grief, no wonder the MOD was vague and hadn't been swamped with volunteers."

"Look, let's get you settled into the mess. It's the old Northern Rhodesia Police mess and it's in town. It's quite decent, actually. There are a few other RAF pilots here, also on loan service, but they aren't QFI's. They are pilots for the ZAF, flying ZAF aeroplanes, until we train up replacements. There are also some pilots and navigators in the ZAF, on contract to the Zambian government, probably ex Rhodesian Air Force crews. You'll be able to tell the difference because we continue to wear RAF hats and have RAF wings on our chests. The contract officers have 100% Zambian uniforms."

Jock drove me into town to the mess in the squadron land rover. Livingstone was not large. It had one main street with a few half decent shops, a cinema, and some quite smart single storey homes. The big, jaw-dropping attraction was the spray from the Victoria Falls, known locally as 'Mosi-Oa-Tunya' (the smoke that thunders), which was about six miles to the south of the town and rose several hundred feet into the air. People would pay money for that view!

As Jock said, the mess was quite decent, and he took me into the bar for a cold beer where we chatted for a couple of hours and he filled me in on all I needed to know about relations between ourselves and the new Zambian government.

It appeared that there was increasing tension between Zambia and the UK on account of the fact that Ian Smith, the Prime Minister of Rhodesia (ex Southern Rhodesia) had declared independence from Britain unilaterally a few weeks before because the British government had refused to grant it to a minority white regime. Britain had punished Rhodesia by stopping oil imports to Rhodesia, whereupon Rhodesia had hijacked the oil coming by train from the port in Mozambique, passing through Rhodesia and destined for Zambia. The net result was that Zambia had very little oil, and that had to come in by air and Rhodesia seemed to have plenty. Another successful operation chalked up by the British government!

The next few months would get quite difficult and the Zambian government applied severe petrol rationing for its population, with the bulk of what little petrol they had going to essential services and the military.

By the time I had bought myself a second-hand car I was issued with petrol coupons for four gallons of petrol, to last six weeks! In time of war, the black-market kicks in. We discovered that we could get a fuel allowance for essential government business to cover exactly the mileage to travel at the rate of consumption of the vehicle.

An official visit to our Air Headquarters in the capital, Lusaka, would clock up over 300 miles from Livingstone. We could therefore claim petrol for six hundred miles for the return journey. However, in this case you would only end up back in Livingstone with the same amount of fuel in the tank as you started with. The solution to the problem was to drive to Lusaka and then to fly the car back to Livingstone on one of our ZAF transport aircraft, the Caribou! So, viola! Three hundred miles worth of buckshee petrol.

As Jock and I *were* the Flying Training School we could make up our own working practices. When we did fly, we had decided that we would start early in the morning, say, 7am and fly until lunchtime at 1pm. In this way we would fly in the cool of the morning and avoid the hot, turbulent afternoons. Much better for basic instruction. We could then go home for the rest of the day and have a barbecue, or a swim or drive down to the Zambesi and watch the elephants and the hippos. We could copy all the flying orders straight from our flying orders used in the RAF, but just leaving out the bits we didn't like. As we were the only QFI's nobody could tell us that there was a better way to do things. This could be a particularly good posting, methinks!

Until we had managed to find a building of our own for the FTS, we would have to share the crew room with the other pilots and navigators in the ZAF. They were as anxious to get rid of us as we were to go and so it wasn't very long before we managed to steal a couple of rooms in the main building for crew rooms, one for us and one for the students, if and when they arrived. We were always on the scrounge for anything to build up our little empire. We were never particularly popular with the 'sitting tenants' because they knew that we were there to train up their replacements.

The ZAF at Livingstone consisted of the two aforementioned chipmunks, several DH Beavers, which were very nice bush aeroplanes, ideally suited to operate in and around Zambia, a couple of Caribous, which flew mainly between Lusaka and Livingstone and a few indeterminate wrecks which sat in a hangar and went nowhere. The last were a gift from Rhodesia! All the aircraft servicing was done by a mixture of RAF loan airmen and the contract airmen.

Jock had decided that, as he was the senior of the two of us, he would be the Chief Flying Instructor (CFI) and I, therefore, would have to be the Chief Ground Instructor (CGI). We would split the ground subjects between us and would divide the students 50/50 for flying, but first we had to get some.

In the event it wasn't very long before our first eight students came along. At that stage we had no part in their selection, but the standard required was, surprisingly, the same as the UK. They had to hold a minimum of five subjects at O level, including maths and English, and be physically fit to the same standards as the UK. This must have been incredibly hard to achieve when you consider that they only needed two O levels to enter their university.

The eight who arrived seemed to be very keen and well educated and were looking forward to flying. Where we noticed a difference between our African students and their British counterparts was that their technical knowledge of what we may think of as common, everyday items, was somewhat lacking due to their limited exposure to technology as children. However, this was offset somewhat by their enthusiasm to learn.

After a few months we were told that there were plans to build a purpose-built Flying Training School building with all our own facilities. This would not happen for several months. We were also making plans to purloin three or four of the Beavers to use as an advanced trainer but, obviously we would need more instructors to fly them.

Of our first students to arrive, two of them showed particular promise. One was a white Northern Rhodesian, Des Arneson, and the other was a very self-assured young man called Philip Lemba. We had been asked by Air Headquarters in Lusaka to try to identify a couple from this first intake who might, after training with us in Livingstone, be able to go to the UK to complete the QFI course at Little Rissington. The plan being that they would then return to Livingstone as true ZAF instructors, eventually to take over from the RAF QFI's (Jock and myself plus any others we might have by then) to continue training their own countrymen. Early signs were that these two students would be suitable and so we would bear that in mind during training.

Zambia lies between about twelve and seventeen degrees to the south of the equator on a high plateau which is around 3,200 feet above sea level in the south, at Livingstone, to over 4,400 further north at Lusaka. Being in the southern hemisphere, therefore, the seasons are reversed from the UK. Summer, which is the rainy season, is between October and March and the Winter, the dry, clear, and cooler season, is from March through to October.

The summer rain, which could be very heavy was interspersed with clearer periods but flying during the afternoons could be very bumpy, hence our decision to fly mornings only. Flying during the cooler clear weather of winter was a delight.

What we did notice straight away was, operating from a high airfield (over 3000 feet), the performance of the chipmunk, not in any way a high-performance aeroplane, was greatly reduced. To climb high enough for aerobatics or spinning would take a lot longer than we were used to.

The Zambesi river which feeds the Victoria Falls flows in from the west to the falls in flat country. At the falls, the water plunges over 300 feet into deep gorges, continuing its flow in these gorges, all the way to the east towards Lake Kariba with its large dam. For this reason, it was a superb landmark for trainee pilots to guide them back to the airfield at Livingstone.

The briefing would be: - 'Fly south until you hit the river. If it is in flat country, turn left and fly until you reach the falls. Livingstone is on your left. If the river is in gorges, then turn right. Fly to the falls and Livingstone is on your right.' They were not to cross the river. South of the Zambesi was Rhodesia and further west it was the border to Bechuanaland (now Botswana).

Both chipmunks were now serviceable, and flight training was soon underway. We managed to send solo six of the first eight students in a reasonable time. We had been asked by the Air Commander in Lusaka (an RAF Group Captain, on loan) not to lower our standards from those we would expect in the RAF but to apply generous latitude in reaching that standard. The Group Captain was not a QFI, but he was certainly a diplomat, possibly essential in working towards a smooth handover to the Zambians.

We tried to explain to him that, if the normal time to solo was around ten to fifteen hours and we stretched that to twenty plus, this, in itself, indicated a lowering of standards. We did, however, understand the position he was in. We, the

RAF, had been tasked with supplying fully trained Zambians to take over the running of the ZAF in due course and, naturally, the Zambian government wanted this to happen yesterday! The problem was that we were starting from zero and these young men, our first students, would constitute all the senior officers of the embryonic Air Force.

It was obvious that not all the students we were sent would make pilots, but they may well still be valuable as senior administrators in the new ZAF. We would therefore not feel quite so bad failing a cadet as a pilot but sending him back to Lusaka to train in some other capacity. They were, after all, very highly educated in comparison to the majority of their countrymen.

I spent my time away from flying looking for a house to rent in the town for when my wife, Hilary, and young Andrew came out after my 25th birthday in February of 1966. I eventually found a two-bedroom bungalow just off the high street which also had a small plunge pool in the garden and was owned by a European contract worker away from Livingstone for several months. We agreed a rent and the property was mine for the duration.

FTS LIVINGSTONE

Training gathered pace when, by the new year of 1966 we had a further two QFI's posted out from the UK. We were now able to spread the load as more students joined to be trained. We were also being included in the initial selection process of these new students.

This might have been brought about after a would-be student on one intake was asked to remove his dark sunglasses during a welcoming address by one of our instructors and found to have only one eye! He, apparently, had completed his initial medical examination in Lusaka. Naturally, he was returned to Lusaka forthwith.

On the lighter side, our involvement in the initial selection of students consisted of vetting the letters of application to join the ZAF written by these would-be trainees.

I really wish that I had kept copies of some of them. However, one of the letters sticks in my mind and caused us a great deal of mirth. The letter rambled on, mostly incoherently, with expressions like, "I have sent the flying eagles to see Mr. Fish's moustache," and ending with, "and , finally, Sirs, I would like to do for Zambia what Napoleon did for Germany."

Surprisingly, our new accommodation was beginning to take shape and it looked as though we might take possession by the time we were ready to move our first students from the basic Chipmunk to the advanced Beaver. This at least would make the Flying Training School look a little more professional.

In early February of 1966 I was told that my wife and son would be arriving out in Lusaka later that month. I had arranged to take a few days away from Livingstone to meet them off the BOAC VC10 when they arrived and to take them to my parents' home in Lusaka for us to spend a few days with them before I took them down to Livingstone. My dad was working on contract for the Zambian Defence Forces as a sergeant major and I teased him that he didn't have to salute me when we were off duty.

After a few days leave in Lusaka I took Hilary and Andrew down to our 'new' house in Livingstone. They seemed to be quite pleased with the bungalow, especially the pool, but we needed to employ a gardener to tend the quite extensive garden, as well as somebody to help with the cleaning in the house.

I was interested to note that we had to apply for any house servants through the local council who would also set the rate of pay – something like £1 per week for a gardener and £12 - £15 per month for a house servant! These rates of pay seemed incredibly low, even allowing for inflation over the years from 1966, but we were told by the local Zambian officials that the rates were set to avoid upsetting the jobs market.

Normally the house servant and his family were accommodated in a little brick house on your property, which most houses seemed to have, and which could easily be mistaken for an outside toilet! We were advised to drip-feed the house servant £1 per week 'ration money' to avoid him taking all his monthly pay in one go and drinking his way through it and taking several days off to recover. Meanwhile, his family would go without food. We developed a system whereby I would drive him down to the milling factory to collect a giant bag of 'mealie meal' (corn flour) to ensure that, whatever happened, his family would have food.

Coming home from flying one day I was met in the driveway by the house servant and Hilary, both of whom seemed to be quite flustered.

"Bwana, there is a dragon in the bedroom!"

Hilary explained that she hadn't seen anything, but the servant was genuinely terrified. She had been on the small terrace by the French windows in the garden with Andrew when he had come running out of the house waving his arms and pointing to the bedroom.

It seemed that I was to be the knight in shining armour so, to look the part, and just in case there were dragons in Zambia, I picked up the dustbin lid for my shield and a garden rake which would serve as my lance.

I entered the house, single storey remember, and advanced, nervously it had to be said, down the short corridor to the main bedroom. Suddenly a huge (if I were a fisherman, I'd say six feet long) monitor lizard came out of the bedroom and stopped dead when it saw me. We both retreated rapidly – me back to the sitting room and the lizard to the bedroom.

Something had to be done by somebody and it appeared that my name was the only one on the list! I crept back down the corridor to the bedroom door and, there, on our bed was the lizard, eyeing the open window just a few inches above his head. I made as if I was going to do something decisive, whereupon the lizard leaped onto the windowsill and launched himself (or herself?) out into the garden and ran past the terrace where a terrified young Andrew, his eyes out on stalks, watched it go.

This would have certain repercussions on Andrew. Months later he started having nightmares about dragons every night and we can only assume it was seeing the lizard jumping out of our window. We told him there were no dragons but why would he believe us? He'd seen one! Coming out of the bedroom!

Dragons aside, life in Livingstone was very pleasant. The local cinema, the Capitol, in the high street was worth a visit from time to time. They actually had the occasional decent film showing but what made a visit worthwhile was the behaviour of the clientele.

No food or drink was sold in the cinema but, next door, there was a bottle shop and general store which stayed open in the evenings whilst a film was showing. There would always be a halftime break which gave the punters time to pop out to the bottle shop to buy a couple of bottles of drink which they would then smuggle back into the cinema. The second half of the film would be punctuated by empty bottles, kicked over on the concrete floor, rolling all the way down to the front of the cinema beneath the seats. It could be hilarious.

The winter season between April and late August was dry with, usually, clear skies and a temperature during the day around the lower 20's. As the winter progressed the land would become more parched and the level of the rivers noticeably lower. This meant that wild game, in particular elephants, would seek out water and could be seen any day of the week along the banks of the Zambesi.

There was a narrow, tarmacked road running along the northern shore of the river, Riverside Drive, and it wasn't at all unusual to drive around a bend and come face-to-face with a large bull elephant crossing the road. Seen up close they are alarmingly big! This is when you discover how fast your car can travel in reverse.

The river itself was home to a large population of hippo's and the occasional crocodile could be seen. There were several beautiful spots for a barbecue between the road and the river and quite often we would spend the late afternoons and early evenings taking advantage of our time away from flying.

Not far along Riverside Drive there was a small game reserve, Livingstone Game Park, which had an amazing number of animals in their natural surroundings. The star attraction was the white rhino with its little baby, but any number of kudu or sable antelope could be seen, not to mention giraffe. There was a large water hole in the park and, as far as I could see, there were no fences so I guess the water must have been the attraction. A drive through the game park was always a popular pastime, especially if you had children in the car.

The Victoria Falls were, of course, spectacular and you could never tire of watching the water cascade over the rim to the gorge below. My only regret was that any RAF loan personnel were prohibited by the British Government to cross the bridge to the other side of the falls into Rhodesia (the outlawed state!) and would therefore miss the, possibly more dramatic, view of the falls from the other side. The silly thing about this ruling was that *anybody* else could make the crossing, including ZAF personnel or, indeed, families of the banned RAF.

Hilary would regularly drive across the falls bridge into the small town of Victoria Falls, Rhodesia, to fill our car up with petrol, unrestricted, whilst in Livingstone we were still severely rationed. She would then be able to go to the hairdressers for an appointment. On many occasions the Rhodesian border guards tried to persuade her to bring me across with her and promised they would not stamp my passport, an offer which I continued to refuse.

Along the Zambesi to the north-west of Livingstone was the small settlement of Mulobesi where the Zambesi Sawmills had a factory employing many Zambians in the cutting and processing of wood. Mulobesi was served by an ancient looking wood burning steam train running from Livingstone. It would transport wood from Mulobesi down to Livingstone where it could be distributed by train throughout Zambia. Any space in the trucks was taken up by employees and their families travelling between Livingstone and Mulobesi.

On one occasion a Zambian employee had been involved in an accident at the sawmill and had been severely injured requiring prompt hospitalisation in the General Hospital at Livingstone. I flew one of our Beavers up to Mulobesi and flew him back to Livingstone with a local medic. The beaver was an ideal aircraft for such emergency evacuations as it could land in any reasonably flat field.

As Winter turned into Spring and then the beginning of Summer the heat and clouds would be gradually building up bringing much more humid conditions. The most unpleasant month was probably October when there was the promise of the first rains after the long dry season but, until the rain actually fell, there was little relief. It was not unusual to see people standing outside in the first of the rains and welcoming a soaking.

At this time of year, the Zambesi was at its lowest level, having not had any rain for several months, and the water over the falls was greatly reduced. This was the time when sightings of herds of elephants crossing the river could be guaranteed. As the rainy season progressed, the river would become higher and the falls more dramatic and, because they were not so desperate for water, elephant sightings would become fewer.

One thing I had not appreciated about Zambia was that from time to time the country would experience earth tremors. I first became aware of this when I was in the garden one day clearing the drive of fallen debris from the trees when I noticed that the corrugated iron roof of our garden tool shed began shaking. I looked up expecting to see an animal, perhaps a monkey, jumping on it, but then it stopped as quickly as it had begun. I was puzzled and I went indoors to tell Hilary about it. She was sitting in an armchair tightly gripping its arms with a terrified look on her face. Before I could say anything, she said,

"Did you feel that? The whole room was 'swimming'!"

I had felt nothing standing in the garden but, in a room, the feeling is more noticeable.

The next time this happened I was sitting in our crew room at the airfield and there was a definite floating sensation and a couple of pieces of furniture moved a few inches. It is quite a weird feeling not knowing if this is suddenly going to become violent and destructive and not really knowing what to do for the best. It just feels as though you are on a boat at sea in a gentle swell.

As 1966 progressed so did the courses we were running at the Flying Training School.

We had sent our two promising students, earmarked for instructor training, to the UK for an advanced flying training course followed by a course at CFS to become instructors. This seemed to be the quickest way to have them trained up and returned to us in a useable form. It was also politically expedient to show the Zambian government that they had two of their own pilots in the system, even if one of them was white.

Towards the year's end we had started the advanced flying course for the students who had reached that stage. The DH Beaver was a more modern and complex aircraft than the Chipmunk, but it was still a single engine propeller aeroplane. It was quite a logical step to use it for the advanced trainer as, when the students qualified with their 'wings', they would fly the self-same Beaver on their first squadron.

The Beaver could carry six soldiers with their equipment, as well as the pilot, and could fly into small strips throughout the country. In fact, one of the exercises we practiced was landing into a small strip up country, usually a suitable farmer's field.

The procedure was to fly low over the 'landing' strip to inspect the surface to make sure it was suitable and there were no potholes. This would also frighten away any wild animals that might be on the strip. We would then land and taxi around for a take-off.

Returning from one such exercise we noticed, ahead of us on the runway at Livingstone, a large snake just after we touched down. We could not avoid it and must have run over it. We did, however, see it try to strike at the aircraft as we passed. I am not sure whether it was hit by the propeller, but we stopped and then backtracked along the runway to where the snake lay, quite still. It turned out to be a black mamba, quite poisonous and quite dead. Cadet pilot, Lungu, and I had a photograph taken with our 'trophy' draped over the propeller.

There continued to be a certain amount of friction between the Zambian and British governments as to whether Zambia should be supplied with fast jets by Britain. Britain resisted, probably mainly on cost, but also that there didn't seem to be any requirement for arming the Zambians with such aircraft. The Zambian argument was that they felt threatened by the breakaway state of Ian Smith's Rhodesia. This was unlikely, as the Rhodesians had their own problems.

The much more likely reason for Zambian requests for modern jets was that other African states had jets, so they felt they needed them to give them a greater presence at the table of independent African states. Also, Dr. Kuanda, the President of the Republic of Zambia, was flying around in an ancient DC3 of 1940's vintage, albeit a beautiful example of the type, when other presidents had smart jets.

This was eventually conceded by the British government and a nice new turbo-prop aircraft was supplied in due course. The fact that it subsequently crashed during a training flight in Lusaka was hugely embarrassing, especially as the dead crew was ex RAF, but the precedent had been set and the president ended up with an aeroplane of which he could be proud.

EXTRA TIME

By April of 1967, my second son, Richard was born. Now we had a true Zambian in the family, and, by his sixteenth birthday, he would have to decide whether he wanted to be British or Zambian! There seemed to be quite a few young children belonging to the RAF loan service personnel and so children's parties were frequent.

We now had six QFI's and the FTS was going on from strength to strength. We were running both basic Chipmunk courses and advanced Beaver courses and we were well settled into our new building. There continued to be rumblings from the Zambians about not having fast jets, but the British government seemed to be sidestepping the arguments quite successfully.

We would get the occasional high-powered visit from Zambian government officials in Lusaka to see if we really were running a Flying Training School and, having satisfied themselves that all was well, would return home and all would go quiet again for several months. It was significant that they would spend considerably more time being wined and dined at their local party headquarters than they would at the FTS.

My landlord let me know that he wanted to take back his property and so I had to make other arrangements. There was a rather splendid two-bedroom government house on the outskirts of town which was conveniently on the road to the airport. I applied and was accepted for this house and we moved in shortly after.

Unfortunately, it didn't have a swimming pool (what was I thinking?) but I came up with a solution to the problem. In town there was a small manufacturer and supplier of farming equipment. I noticed that he made water tanks of corrugated galvanised steel and would make one to my specification. I asked for a tank twelve feet diameter, four feet deep with no top and a drain hole in the base. He was bemused when I told him I wanted it as a splash pool for the kids, but he made it, nonetheless.

By the time he delivered it to the property my gardener had dug a hole into which the tank would fit neatly. Fortunately for the gardener the soil was very sandy and easy to dig. He certainly earned his £1 per week this time! All I had to do now was to set paving stones around it and erect a safety fence.

The route from our new house to the airport was up a long straight gradient for a couple of miles passing heavily wooded areas on both sides of the road. I had bought a small Japanese fold-up motorbike which was light on petrol and therefore useful in a time of rationing. I used this for the journey to work but, quite often, on the road I would pass troops of baboons crossing the road who seemed to be completely uninterested in this human on a strange machine travelling flat-out at 15mph.

Life now continued in the same easy-going manner that we had become used to, with flying in the morning and the rest of the day off to barbecue on the banks of the Zambesi, watching the wild game.

Just along Riverside Drive there was a small and mainly overgrown burial ground. The gravestones, when you could find them, showed the names of the early Europeans, some with their families, who died in the area after David Livingstone had discovered the falls. They were all young and none died of natural causes, the main killer being blackwater fever (a complication of malaria). There were one or two who died after accidents – 'killed by falling rocks at the falls.' It was very sobering to think that less than a hundred years before, this area was so hazardous to these first explorers and their families.

Into 1968 I was approaching the point at which, having completed my two and a half years on my tour, I would be going back to the UK. Again, I could put in my preferences, but as I would only have just over two years to serve before my twelve-year engagement was up it seemed like it might be 'Hobson's Choice.' On the other hand, I could ask to continue in Zambia which would see my time out.

I knew that the RAF still had difficulty in filling the QFI slots in Zambia. Loan service was not everybody's cup of tea as, in truth, you dropped off the RAF radar which would not help if this was a lifetime career. It was certainly worth a try even though some of my friends in Livingstone thought I was mad to go for another round.

The first of April 1968 saw the 50th anniversary of the founding of the Royal Air Force. It was the world's oldest air force, and we were determined to celebrate it. We arranged a celebration dinner in a local restaurant in Livingstone and all current and ex RAF personnel living locally were invited.

Where we made our mistake was not inviting any local dignitaries. We assumed that they wouldn't be interested. However, we had not considered the political aspect of this. It was reported in the local press that a group of white racists had gathered for a political rally. We continued to get a lot of bad press for this, but they were not interested in our reasoning, so we just had to ride it out.

Meanwhile I was accepted for a second posting, but I insisted that I and my family would be given a couple of weeks leave in the UK between the back-to-back postings. MOD agreed. They would have to give me that leave anyway between any two postings and they would also have to transport out any replacement QFI and his family, so they were no worse off.

With a bit of fast talking, I even managed to get them to agree to transport out a couple of crates of my 'belongings' to Zambia. Again, they would have to do that for a replacement. I could then shop in the UK for things which I knew we couldn't get in Zambia, e.g., good children's clothes from M&S in varying sizes for growing children.

After a very pleasant couple of weeks staying with Hilary's parents in Poole and nailing down a couple of crates full of goodies for the family whilst we were in Zambia, we set off back to Livingstone.

Nothing had changed. Same house, same FTS, even the same instructors. Now, with just two years to serve in the RAF I could bring my mind to bear on what the future might hold for me at the end of my service.

I had decided that I would like to go into civil aviation. I would have the time to start studying for my ATPL exams so that I could approach a possible future employer with the correct licences. I even managed to get our RAF Education Officer, Derek Johnson, to have the Service pick up the tab for my ATPL correspondence course which I could now work my way through at my leisure.

Not very far to the west of Livingstone was a small settlement called Kazungula on the banks of the Zambezi. At this point there was a very Heath-Robinson looking car ferry which seemed to be using numerous biscuit tins for flotation but, if you could summon up the courage to use it, you could cross into Bechuanaland, a British Protectorate, which still had a splendid union Jack fluttering from the flagpole outside the local police station on the other side of the river. It was now just a short drive to a small hotel on the banks of the Chobe river, a subsidiary of the Zambesi, and the entrance to the Chobe Game Reserve. This was well worth a few days visit as, even to this day, this area of Botswana, as it now is, has the largest number of elephants in the whole of Africa.

Game viewing drives from the hotel into the game reserve were well worth taking provided you understood what you were in for. The game warden driving you was determined to scare the living daylights out of you by persuading an angry bull elephant to chase the Land Rover.

By this time, back in Livingstone, we had trained several Zambian students up to the point of receiving their wings. We felt it might be a good idea to try to get the President of Zambia to come down to Livingstone to pin the wings on to his first pilots' breasts. The Air Commander in Lusaka thought this might be a good idea and so the invitation was issued by him and accepted by the Office of the President.

We could now go ahead and organise the parade and even a mini fly-past over the parade ground. The Officers' Mess in Livingstone could prepare a special lunch and there would be official photographs taken of the President and his staff with all the QFI's and the newly 'winged' students. It was hoped that this might go some way towards silencing the voices in the Zambian government calling for the dismissal of the RAF in favour of a friendly power who might be able to promise them the fast jets they so craved.

The day went as well as we could have hoped for. The parade was quite impressive; the successful students received their wings and even the flypast of four chipmunks, a couple of beavers and a caribou looked quite tidy. The cherry on the cake though was when we managed to persuade the president to fly as a passenger in a beaver flown by the first Zambian pilot, Philip Lemba, now a fully trained QFI. The look on the president's face as they taxied out for take-off must have been like mine when we were chased by the elephant.

By January of 1969, my third son Michael was born, so we now had a second Zambian member of the family. The tin swimming pool really came into its own that year as ours was not the only family increasing in size. There seemed to be birthday parties most months.

We soon received the news that the Zambian government had agreed a deal with the Italian Air Force to take over the training of Zambian pilots and we were to complete a handover of the FTS, lock, stock, and barrel to the Italians when they arrived later in the year. What we didn't know at that time was that the first batch of Italian instructors, a) could not speak English and, b) had never flown a propeller driven aeroplane in their lives. We therefore were given the task of 'converting' them to the chipmunk and the beaver when they arrived.

On the day of their arrival the RAF contingent were lined up on the concrete pad outside the FTS buildings ready to receive our replacements. The Italian Air Force transport aircraft stopped in front of us and half a dozen pilots of the Italian Air Force descended the steps and walked towards us. It brought to my mind the meeting of Jock Byrne and myself nearly four years before and I wondered whether it would be appreciated if I tried the, "Dr. Livingstone, I presume?" introduction. I decided against it as, if they couldn't speak English, maybe they wouldn't understand English humour!

Over the next few weeks, we discovered that most of their instructors did have a smattering of English but their commander could speak the language very well, so all was not lost. However, it was rather amusing to teach them the vagaries of flying a prop aeroplane with its gyroscopic swing effect on take-off as compared with the reasonably straight forward handling of the jet. Still, maybe they could bring their jets in sooner rather than later.

END IN SIGHT

By this time, I was going through the end of tour procedure which I had experienced a few times before.   We were told that because we were being 'short toured' and returning to UK early MOD would give us special consideration for our next posting. (!) We were required, as usual, to give our preferences.

I realised that because I had less than a year to serve in the RAF, I could hardly expect an attractive posting. It was important to me that I kept my flying current as I would be looking to Join an airline, so I tried to be realistic. My choices were: -

A Flying tour in the South of England.

A Flying tour anywhere.

A ground tour in the south of England.

Naturally, the RAF came up trumps and gave me a ground tour in the north of England! I was to be an Operations Officer at one of our front-line fighter stations in northern Lincolnshire.

My job would be one of a team of Ops Officers to coordinate between Strike Ops Headquarters and the fighter squadrons on the station. We had to keep HQ updated at all times of the strength and serviceability of the aircraft on the squadrons. It was a 24 hour a day job and there was a little bedroom in the Ops block for our use. As this was the height of the cold war, we had to be able to scramble the fighters in the event of an airborne threat from the east. To this end we had to make sure the airfield was always open. If there was a snowstorm, we had to call out the snow ploughs.

Whilst this was a serious job, I have to admit to feeling a little frustrated that I couldn't keep my flying up to date nor could I be in the south where I needed to be to take my licence exams. I would also need to 'buy' some flying on a twin-engine aircraft to take my instrument rating flight with the CAA and that was going to cost me a sizeable chunk of my RAF gratuity awarded after my twelve years' service. I found a small airfield, Stapleford Tawney, near Stansted where I could fly the several hours required on a twin Apache for the rating.

I had approached my new boss and told him that, as I was leaving the Service, I would be taking my four weeks terminal leave. On top of that I still had three weeks annual leave owing to me which I intended to take immediately before my terminal leave. He was furious! He told me I was placing an unnecessary load on the remaining ops officers and he wanted me to reconsider my request. I told him I was sorry for the rest of the team but that I was taking my entitlement and that the MOD were well aware of this entitlement and should have supplied the necessary staff to take this into account. I had, after all, given him a few months' notice and so there was plenty of time to replace me.

When the time came for me to leave my boss didn't give me a gold watch or even a farewell and good luck card, but I still rode into the sunset with, I have to admit, some regrets for leaving what had been a good twelve year stint in some very interesting places. Oh, and they had taught me to fly!

I intended to use my leave to organise and take my exams for the Air Transport Pilots' Licence and to arrange my flying for the instrument rating at Stapleford Tawney. Meanwhile, I would apply to BEA and BOAC for the all-important flying job. Whilst I was still on leave with the RAF my family could still stay in our married quarter on the station, but my service ended on 1st. October 1970 by which time we would need to find other accommodation. It was therefore important that, by then, I had taken all my exams, including the flying, and had an acceptance of a job. We could then spend some time looking for a house.

FLT/LT TO MR.

The time had come for me to leave the soft bosom of the RAF which had been my home since leaving school.

I had signed on for twelve years with the option of leaving after eight, but I had not taken that option which, with hindsight, was possibly not the best decision. It's true to say that those last four years in the RAF were very enjoyable but I would find that delaying my entry into civil aviation would adversely impact my future career by adding, possibly, at least eight years to my time to command.

I was to find out that flying for most civil airlines was a numbers game and, provided you reached the appropriate standards, promotion and opportunity depended upon your date of joining not on your experience. Unlike some occupations where a final pension would depend upon the position or status achieved in the company, with most airlines it was based upon time served as well as final rank achieved. There could be a world of difference between walking through the entry door of the airline at the head of a long queue of applicants and being at the tail end.

I had spent the last few months in the Service studying for my ATPL (Airline Transport Pilot's Licence) and would need to pass these exams to obtain a licence which would enable me to apply for a position as a pilot in an airline. This was an essential step as no amount of RAF flying could exempt you from these exams but a flying test to demonstrate your ability to fly was not required. You did, however, need to take an instrument flight rating, to be examined by a pilot of the CAFU (Civil Aviation Flying Unit) before you could be awarded an Instrument Rating to validate your new ATPL.

Having spent a good proportion of my flying overseas I had been quite keen to fly for an overseas airline. I had written to Cathay Pacific who had wanted more recent multi-jet experience than I had; South African Airways who had wanted me to be bi-lingual in English and Afrikaans, and various others who weren't interested for one reason or another. As a back-up I had written to BEA (British European Airways) and BOAC (British Overseas Airways Corporation). Both had asked me to attend for an interview.

The interview with BOAC had been interesting.

I had travelled down from Lincolnshire the evening before the interview at Heathrow and stayed in a hotel at the airport to be on site for the following morning. I had charged BOAC the £5 B&B charge, as I had been told to do, and presented myself to the secretary for the interview with a senior management pilot. I had my flying logbooks with me in case they wanted to inspect them.

Apparently, I was to have two interviews, both by senior management pilots, one after the other. This turned out to be a bit like 'Good Cop, Bad Cop' scenario. The first gentleman was very friendly. It turned out that he had been in the RAF years before. We spent the whole interview talking about my flying in the RAF and he was a real 'uncle' character. He ended by saying, "I see you were a QFI in the Air Force. Well, I'm sure that will come in useful during your future career in BOAC." He wished me good luck and said that he was looking forward to seeing me again.

The second pilot was quite different. He came across as being brusque and unfriendly and fired a lot of technical questions at me. He was also critical of my having spent £5 of the airline's money on the hotel the previous night, implying that I could have found somewhere cheaper. I told him that, as an RAF officer I believed I had behaved honourably. He seemed to be going out of his way to unbalance me. However, we made it to the end of the interview with him saying, "I see you were a QFI in the RAF. Well, you needn't think that will do you any good in your career with BOAC." It was difficult not to laugh as I was dismissed.

I subsequently received a letter of acceptance from BOAC, conditional upon my passing my Instrument Rating flying Exam, which I was waiting to take in a few weeks. Without passing that I would have a Commercial Pilot's Licence only and not the full ATPL.

I did not rush to accept the offer from BOAC as I had an interview with BEA in a few days' time and wanted to know what they would say. My preference was to fly for the Long-Haul BOAC rather than the Short-Haul BEA, but I needed to hedge my bets in case I failed to get my Instrument Rating.

The interview with BEA was on a different level entirely. For a start, there was only one interview with a panel of senior figures, comprising two pilots, an engineer, a doctor and a.n.other.

It was very easy going and it appeared that they had already decided that I would be offered a job. They did ask me if I had been to see 'the opposition' (BOAC). I told them that, honestly, I had. They asked if they might ask the outcome of that interview. I told them that I had been offered a position dependent upon my having an ATPL.

They looked at each other and said they would offer me a job with what I had at that moment – a Commercial Pilot's Licence. It would seem rude to tell them that I really only wanted to fly for BOAC and so I thanked them and said I would let them know.

I did feel a little awkward about that as it seemed terribly ungrateful not to accept their kind offer there and then. I tried to look pleased, but it would have been so much better had they made the offer by letter so they couldn't see my reaction. They even asked one of the pilots on the panel to show me around the crew's reporting room in the Queen's Building where, they said, I would probably bump into some of my old RAF pals.

Next, I had to write to BOAC and tell them that I had been offered a job with BEA with the licence that I held at that time, the CPL, but that my preference was to join BOAC so where did I stand? They replied by return that they, also, would offer me a position with just the CPL but, in my own interests, it would serve me to join with the ATPL and they had every confidence that I would achieve this.

Great! I could now thank BEA very nicely but turn them down. I was on track to become a long-haul pilot.

I did, in fact, pass my Instrument Rating flight with the CAA flying a twin-engine Apache propeller aircraft out of Stanstead. I had to fly several hours in the aircraft, based at Stapleford Tawney, before taking the test and to pay, not only for the aircraft, but also for the instruction, which cost me a sizeable chunk of my RAF gratuity paid for my 12 years' service. However, that was the price for a job!

The flight test itself was very comprehensive. Naturally, it was all on instruments and consisted of a take-off and published instrument departure from Stansted followed by a short cross country on airways leading to an instrument approach to the runway at Stansted. This led to a go-around during which an engine was failed on me and a further approach on one engine to a final instrument landing.

Taxying in to park the examiner was not forthcoming, only giving me instructions to park the aircraft. There then followed a lengthy debriefing of the whole flight at the end of which he congratulated me and said that I had passed the rating and he had enjoyed flying with me.

When I showed surprise he said, "Well, if I had told you before the debriefing that you had passed, you probably wouldn't have listened to another word I said, so I have learned that this is the best way to hold your attention."

I was now able to accept the job offer from BOAC and to tell them that I had an ATPL.

They gave me a date, the 14th of September to start my course with them at their training school at Cranebank, on the eastern side of Heathrow.

CRANEBANK

In the first few days of September 1970 we had managed to find a new house on the outskirts of Reading which we were able to move into before the start of my new job on 14th of the month.

I was pleased that the transition from the RAF to the civil world was turning out to be relatively stress-free. In fact, whilst I would be on the payroll of BOAC from 14th September I would still be on terminal leave with the RAF and receiving service pay until the end of the month. Two jobs, two pay packets for two weeks!

On day one at Cranebank all the new intake was assembled for the usual introductory talk by a senior manager. I could see that there were several ex-RAF pilots joining as well as a sprinkling of pilots from other airlines.

By this time, I was approaching my 30th birthday but I could see that there were a few much younger pilots who were joining direct from the Air Training College at Hamble which was a joint Training school run by BOAC and BEA to supply pilots for both airlines without having to rely on the Services. They would have been in their early 20's.

We would be split into two courses: one to join the Boeing 707 fleet and the other to fly the VC10. Generally, the more experienced pilots would go to the 707 and those with the least flying experience would be put on the VC10 course. Being ex RAF, and with an ATPL, I was destined to go to the

707. We were told that there would be no changes, and the management decision would be final.

I was not particularly enamoured with the idea of flying the 707; the VC10 had always held a fascination for me and, had I been given a choice, would have chosen it. With one exception, there were no dissenters. One pilot, who had been scheduled for the VC10, had approached the manager, and bluntly told him that, unless he could join the 707 fleet he would leave.

Now the thinking was, at that time, that the Boeing 707 was the ubiquitous airliner whilst only BOAC was flying the VC10. If you were to fail the 707 course with BOAC, you could apply to almost any other airline flying 707's whereas failing the VC10 course would leave you stranded. The answer was, don't fail the course!

We, on the 707, were asked if there was anybody who would be prepared to swap to the VC10. Naturally, I raised my hand and was transferred to the VC10 forthwith.

The course at Cranebank lasted several weeks and consisted of a very comprehensive ground school covering all the technical aspects and systems of the VC10 and an introduction to flying the aeroplane by means of the simulator.

At that time, the simulators were considered to be cutting edge and we were all duly impressed. With hindsight, however, they were pretty basic. The instrumentation inside was very representative of the aircraft, and the hydraulic movement built into the machine was quite impressive.

All of the drills and emergencies could be realistically practiced but the visual presentation out of the front screen was a bit like 'Thunderbirds' on TV. In fact, in a large room next to the simulator was a huge model of the countryside, built on a wall, with a runway at the end of it. A TV camera would travel across the model synchronised with the flight of the simulator and this image would be presented to the pilots through their flight deck windscreens. All this was managed, sometimes less than satisfactorily, and through no fault of his own, by a gentleman sitting at a desk in this next room. We had to endure frequent breakdowns but in 1970 this was as good as it got!

All the exams on the technical side were conducted in house by the airline. The CAA had accepted that the national 'flag carrier' was completely trustworthy in the setting and marking of the exams and so were able to sign licences as approved by the Authority.

By the time we were ready to be introduced to the aeroplane proper, we had passed our ARB (Air Registration Board) exam for the VC10 and, Provisional upon passing our flying training, would have the VC10 signed into our licences.

The 'base' flying was conducted, mainly, at Shannon airport on the west coast of Ireland. This was an international airport built specifically for transatlantic traffic which would stop there to refuel prior to the Atlantic crossing. By the time the airport was built the traffic had the range to fly direct from London or the continent to the USA without needing to land in Ireland. It was, therefore, ideal for our needs. It had all the equipment of a modern international airport with none of the traffic. We could fly circuits around it to our heart's content, and we did. The Irish were pleased to see us there because, who else was going to use the place?

In the early part of 1971, we had finished training and our licences had been signed up showing that we were qualified as P1 (First Pilot) on the VC10 with an instrument rating. We were now ready to fly in the aeroplane with real passengers!

VC10 FLEET

B y the time I was ready for my first flight I had collected my new uniform (with one ring on each sleeve) and my two military medals which, if we had them, we were encouraged to wear by the airline. Mine were General Service Medals from my flying in Borneo with 45 Sqn. during the Confrontation with Indonesia. The single ring of rank designated me as a Second Officer which I would have to wear for my first six months in the airline. Whilst my rank was Second Officer, my position on the aircraft was P3, or third pilot.

The normal length of time for a second officer was two years but my previous RAF hours entitled me to a reduction of 18 months. As a P3 I would be basically under instruction when flying the routes on scheduled services.

The flight crew on the VC10 was a captain, a co-pilot, a flight engineer and, on some sectors, a navigator. All the pilots' licences were the same; we were all signed off as P1. That meant, from a licence point of view, we were all entitled to fly as the pilot-in-charge of the aircraft, having passed the same flight tests as each other. This was common sense and allowed any pilot to take over in an emergency.

It was quite usual, and indeed encouraged, for the captain to 'give' the sector away to any of the other pilots. In doing so they would have to make all the decisions regarding fuel and the conducting of the flight as if they were the captain. In this way a crew member would build up valuable experience for when his time came to take command. He would also be encouraged to make any p.a. announcements to the passengers. In other words, the ship was his.

My first scheduled flight was to Hong Kong via Tel Aviv with a night stop in Teheran and then a further night stop in Bangkok before flying to Hong Kong. Our return took us through Calcutta to Teheran and then back to London. Although I wasn't given any of the sectors on this, my first scheduled service flight, I did spend a large amount of the time in the co-pilot's seat.

From the next flight and thereafter, I spent more time actually flying the aircraft and accumulating the knowledge necessary for a competent VC10 pilot. It was rare not to be given at least one sector on a trip.

By March 1971 I had served six months in the airline and collected my second ring on my sleeves and was, therefore, a First Officer.

Shortly after this Hilary, the boys and I moved to a house in Farnham Common, South Buckinghamshire, where my commute to the airport would be easier. It was a more up-market area than where we had been in Caversham, near Reading, and the schools in the area were very highly thought of. Our previous house was never going to be our permanent home, just a stopgap after leaving the RAF.

During the whole of 1971 I continued to fly wherever the routes took us, all the while building up time and experience in the co-pilot's seat. The one exception was that we were not allowed to fly into the USA for our first year of operation. The US Air Traffic Control system was considered to be too much of a challenge for a novice pilot (!) and so I would not get to fly into the States until early 1972. Wow!

However, by mid-1972 I was put on the Navigation course which would require another few weeks in Cranebank sitting in front of the screen of the navigation trainers – a clever box of tricks which enabled you to simulate astro-navigation star shots.

The aim of the course was for you, as a junior pilot, to obtain a Flight Navigator's Licence to navigate the aircraft in those parts of the world, or over ocean, where navigation aids were few and far between.

Some years before, BOAC had employed actual flight navigators for this task. They were not pilots and could not, therefore, be used in any other capacity than navigation. It occurred to the Company that money could be saved, and greater flexibility enjoyed by making their pilots, other than their captains, flight navigators as well as pilots. This meant that any pilots joining BOAC would now, after a period of flying as a pilot, be scheduled to take the navigation course with the aim of achieving the licence. They could then be used in either capacity, even on the same trip.

This was not an easy course and was not universally popular amongst junior pilots. It required a certain dexterity with mathematics and had the inconvenience of not being able to use the calculator, which was not on the market at that time.

With my poor record of maths at school, thanks to a very unfriendly maths teacher, I was concerned that I might not make the grade. However, the Company had a way of helping you through the course.

On day one, the Navigation Instructor said that he was aware of the bad name the course had amongst pilots, but they had come up with a way of helping us pass.

"It's quite simple," he said, "If you don't pass, you're out of a job." That worked, strangely enough.

It was a tough course and more than once I heard myself asking divine forgiveness for all the nasty things I had said about navigators over the years. Having said that, when you had a Navigator's licence there was something rather special about knowing that you were the only one on the flight deck who *definitely* knew you were lost!

It continues to be a source of wonder to me, even now, that we were able to navigate an aeroplane flying at over 500 hundred miles per hour using a sextant to take position lines from a selection of stars. I feel that, perhaps, I should have sent my old maths teacher a photograph of my nav. licence and say, "There you are, mate!"

Taking star shots was concentrated work. All those not interested in astro navigation, look away now!

The sextant we used was of the periscopic type and, as such, was mounted in the roof of the flight deck through an airlock mechanism allowing it to poke up through the roof into the outside air. As the aircraft was bumping around somewhat the 'shot' of the star was captured over a two-minute period with a wind-up clockwork motor on the sextant in order to 'average out' the bumps. In this way, if the shot were started at, say, 12.04 the star would continue to be held in the centre viewing spot until 12.06. The elevation of the star would, by averaging out, be that at 12.05. With the appropriate arithmetic a position line could be produced for 12.05 and drawn on the chart. However, a single position line would not be particularly useful. You needed two more, preferably at 120 degrees to each other.

You would then need to start your shot on the second star at 12.08, finishing at 12.10 for a position line at 12.09. The same for the third star at 12.12, finishing at 12.14 for the third position line at 12.13. You can see that there are only two minutes between finishing one shot and starting the next. In that two minutes you must take the reading off the sextant, do the maths to produce a position line which then needs to be drawn on the chart. The sextant now must be set up for the next star, once it has been identified through the eyepiece, ready to start the shot. Having taken all three shots successfully you now have three position lines on the chart approximately 120 degrees from each other.

However, these are for three different times and you need them for the same time. The way to do this is to transfer the first line along the aircraft track for eight minutes at the aircraft's current estimated ground speed and the second one for four minutes. This should, if you are lucky, give you three lines crossing at a point which is your position at 12.13.

But time has passed and that was your position then. You then must progress along your chart in the direction you were actually flying to a time when you will make a correction to return to the desired track. Now then, class, are you with me so far?

You pass the new heading to the pilot to return to track and the time he should make this correction. All you have to do then is to estimate when you will be back on track and the new heading to maintain this from the data you have discovered from your last position report and tell the pilot. Don't take any time off yet, you are going to be doing this again either at 40-minute cycles or, if you are really fast, at 20-minute cycles.

I am reminded of a sector I was navigating between Singapore and Darwin, en-route to Sydney. I had set up my chart and made ready the sextant for my first series of three-star shots. When you are standing at the sextant on the VC10 you are standing near the entrance door to the flight deck in the centre of the passageway. When the door opens, perhaps with a fresh supply of tea, you can be clearly seen by the first-class passengers.

On this occasion the stewardess from first class said that there was a passenger in first who was very interested in navigation and had seen me using the sextant and wondered if he could come and talk to me about it.

My *second* answer was, "Oh, all right then," (looking at my watch) "but bring him up seven minutes from now and take him away in ten minutes from now as I'm in the middle of star shots."

I had already decided that I didn't really have time to chat to him so I would just run through the procedure of taking the shots and transferring it to the chart and all that followed.

I imagined, as he was 'interested' in navigation, it may well have been that he knew a considerable amount about the procedure. Perhaps he had a boat and had used astro himself. I gave him the whole nav. course in about two minutes.

I got to the end of my rapid explanation, including the chart and the Air Almanac, and said, I thought, kindly,

"Any questions?" To which he replied, "Er, watcha mean, degrees?"

747 'JUMBO'

Early in 1975 I had decided that I needed to move to the 747. The aircraft was taking more and more of the routes which used to be flown by the VC10 and the 707 and this was the main workhorse of the new British Airways.

In 1974 BOAC and BEA had combined to form British Airways and it was obvious that, before long, ex BEA pilots on the new combined list, more senior than myself, would be transferring to the 747 and I might lose my chance.

I was accepted for transfer and by April started the conversion course at Cranebank.

It was more of the same, really. Ground school for the technical side and into the simulator (very smart by VC10 standards) for the flying. No Thunderbirds models for the visual system and virtually everything could be covered on the syllabus without looking at an aeroplane. There was, however, still some base flying required and that, in our case, was flown at Prestwick in Scotland.

By the beginning of October, I was qualified and back on the routes in the 747.

It was a lovely aeroplane to fly and I felt truly fortunate to be on an aircraft which most pilots in the world would love to have on their licences.

We carried only the two pilots and a flight engineer. There was no need for a navigator as this aeroplane had a built-in inertial nav. system which just had to be programmed for the appropriate route. Much as I had enjoyed the challenge of plotting our progress on a chart using the stars on VC10's this was really quite cutting edge.

The routes we flew on the 747 were becoming more attractive as the VC10 and the 707 were scaled down. The Jumbo was now flying regularly to Australia via the Middle East and Singapore. On this route it was in direct competition with Qantas, the Australian Flag Carrier, but was suffering problems at the Australian end of the route because London based crews, being out of their time zone in Australia, had a shorter working duty day than the locally based Qantas crews. This became a problem if there were any delays due to unserviceability of an aircraft when BA crews would go out of hours sooner than the Qantas crews.

BA decided that the answer was to base some crews in Australia. They would make it a voluntary three month posting and would man the base with twelve flight deck crews being twelve each of captains, co-pilots, and flight engineers. The plan was that these crews would operate between Australia, New Zealand, and South-East Asia whilst the usual London based crews would operate the rest of the route. If there was a problem at the far end of the route the Australia based crews would have a longer duty day allowable and, if a crew needed to be replaced, there would be another available. This would then, it was hoped, wipe out the advantage that Qantas had, who, incidentally, had crews based in London.

These postings were quite popular, especially during our winter and, therefore, the Australian summer. The company would book the crews into the local contracted hotel or, would pay the individuals the equivalent allowance to make their own arrangements. Almost invariably this was what most crew members chose depending on whether they had family members on the posting with them. Although these postings were desirable there were many crew members who could not volunteer because of children's schooling, etc. so generally it was not hard to get one.

I was accepted for one in mid-1977. At that time, the posting was in Melbourne and I decided, because I was unaccompanied, the children being at school in the UK, that I would find my own pad. I found a quite respectable self-contained apartment above a pub. I discussed with the landlord how I was to access my rooms outside pub hours. No problem. He gave me a key to the front door.

The pub was only a hundred yards or so down the road from the 'official' crew hotel. When I was due to go out on service, invariably when the pub was closed, I would leave my suitcase in the hall of the pub and walk down to the hotel to get into our taxi for the Flight crew. I would ask the driver to stop at the pub on his way to the airport so I could get my case. His eyes were out on stalks. This had been the most impressive thing this true Aussie had ever seen. "How the hell did yuh git a kay to the pub?"

After a month or so of the posting my family came out and I managed to find some suitable accommodation about 40 miles to the south of the city in Mount Martha on the Mornington peninsula. This was really on the limit of my distance from the airport which was on the far side of the city. I had to make sure I was within an hour and a half from the airport in case I was called out. It was stretching it a bit, but it was a lovely area. We even managed to get the boys into a local school, more to give them the experience of an Australian school than to continue their education.

After a while I discovered that a few of the guys were living in Sydney, a much more attractive place to be. I wondered how they could make themselves available to be within an hour and a half of the airport at Melbourne when they were on standby. It was quite clever, really. The BA aircraft that they were covering for would transit Sydney for Melbourne before turning round and flying back via Sydney northbound. They would hitch a ride on the aircraft from Sydney, stay with it in Melbourne and get off again when it landed at Sydney on its way home. They would therefore be instantly available should they be required.

As soon as I found this out, I drove the family up to Sydney where we spent the rest of the posting.

I managed a second posting in 1979 but by this time the posting was officially in Sydney. I think the company had seen the light. This time I found a flat near the beach in Manly over the harbour from the city and would take the ferry to be picked up near Circular Quay to be taken to the airport. The BA flight from London landed in Sydney early in the morning so coming home to Manly meant taking an early morning ferry across the beautiful harbour and, in the early morning sunshine, drinking a cold beer, having first divested myself of all my BA badges and epaulettes, and looking forward to throwing myself into bed. I had now served a few years as a First Officer, with two rings on my sleeve, but had now been promoted to Senior First Officer, with three rings on each sleeve.

Some months later, after the posting, whilst on a flight out of London, the captain on my trip happened to be the Flight Training Manager. He asked me why, considering my background as a QFI, I had never applied to join the training section as a training first officer. I had to smile thinking back to my interview for BOAC. I couldn't really give him a convincing answer, but he told me that they were currently recruiting, and he would be disappointed not to see my name on the list of applicants. Hence, my name appeared on the list.

Within a couple of months, I had endured the interviews and been accepted. This was followed by a course on instructional techniques and then several hours training in the simulator. As a trainer, you not only had to watch and mark the performance of the crews under test but also how to operate the simulator for that particular flight profile and the failures to be fed in. You would also be required to do a reduced amount of normal route flying fed into your training schedule to keep your licence current.

In the airline each crew member had to fly two simulator details each six months under test conditions to keep their flight licence valid. Any and every conceivable failure would be fed into the machine and the only acceptable result was a total pass. Any failure would require you to retake the test. On top of this was, of course, the strict annual medical.

At the time I was recruited into the training section there was a (flexible) limit of three years as a training first officer after which time you would return to normal route flying. The feeling at that time was that the option of spending time as a trainer was sufficiently valuable that it should be shared amongst the first officer community. Consequently, in 1983 I left the training section and found myself fully back on route flying.

1983 was a turbulent year for Hilary and me. The marriage was showing a great deal of strain. In fact, it had been doing so for several years, but we had ridden out the rough spots for the sake of the boys, but things were now coming to a head. Hilary had taken various courses at the local college and was determined to go into business before it was too late. After some incredibly stressful months we had decided to separate. The boys would continue to live with me in the family home and Hilary would move out. I felt that I would be able to cope, certainly whilst I was at home, and the boys were old enough to manage whilst I was away, provided I did not fly long trips. I would fill the freezer with individual meals which they could each choose and heat in the microwave. There was a school bus which left from the end of our road so, for short periods, they could cope without me. We also had some exceptionally reliable and caring next-door neighbours who had been part of our lives for many years and would be there for emergencies. This actually worked out quite well for several months, but it was whilst I was out researching appropriate dishes for the boys' individual meals that I met (and subsequently fell in love with) Rita, who would eventually become my wife. The date was Friday 13th January 1984.

Rita was divorced and had a son, Fraser, of thirteen and a daughter, Tania, of eleven. My boys were nineteen, seventeen and fifteen. I visited Rita as often as I could in Ascot to where she had just moved but we both had the commitment of spending as much time as possible with our children.

Two and a half years after we met, Rita sold her house and she and her children moved in with me in Farnham Common. My eldest son, Andrew, had a share in a small house near Slough and my youngest, Michael, moved out to live with Hilary. The rest of us muddled along together but it was difficult for Rita's children as they had quite a distance to travel to their schools in Windsor. At about this time my divorce from Hilary had come through and I felt somewhat easier about the relationship between Rita and myself. I declared Rita and her two children to BA as part of my family so that I could take them on the occasional trip with me.

On 28th September 1987 it was going to be Rita's 40th birthday. I knew that she had always admired the Concorde and would look up into the sky to watch it as it flew out of Heathrow. She had also never been to New York and I found I had the opportunity to combine both passions. Her birthday fell on the Monday so, without telling her what I had planned, I asked her if she could arrange to have a few days off from work. At the time she worked for Lotus Software in Staines and she had a very understanding boss. Of course, I had to tell her that we were going away for a few days but wouldn't tell her where.

On the Friday morning we drove into Heathrow and, as we approached the airport, a Concorde took off and passed overhead. Rita looked up through the sunroof and said, "Oh, just look at that…. Beautiful!" I felt I had got this one right.

In the terminal I took the tickets from my pocket (you remember when we had paper tickets?). They had 'Concorde' printed across the front. I passed them to Rita to hold and her face was an absolute picture. She squealed with delight. She could hardly contain herself as we checked in at the special Concorde desk and then passed to the Concorde lounge.

We boarded the aircraft and sat in our allocated seats. It was amazing just how small the cabin was compared to the 747 but, hey, who's complaining? The seats were real leather!

After the exhilarating take-off and climb the aircraft flew out over the Bristol channel and accelerated towards Mach 2 – twice the speed of sound. At the front of the passenger cabin there is a speed readout showing the current Mach number.

It was an absolute co-incidence that I knew the co-pilot on the aircraft, and I arranged that we went up to the flight deck once we were out over the Atlantic to see the crew. I had been on the same conversion course to the 747 with the co-pilot before he transferred to the Concorde. They asked if I would like to come up with them for the landing into New York. Of course, I would have loved to, but I told them it was Rita's birthday and asked if she could come up instead of me. They could hardly refuse. So, to this day, she can tell whoever may be interested that she has been on the flight deck of Concorde whilst it landed in New York!

We managed to travel into the city with the flight crew in their transport as we would be staying in the same hotel. When I picked up the key to our room and passed it to the elderly bell hop to take our cases up, he looked at it and said, "Hell, we can do better than that." He changed it at the desk and took us to the most amazing room with a view right along 6th Avenue.

The rest of the weekend was magic. We had a carriage ride around Central Park. We took a helicopter flight over Manhattan. We visited Macy's and Bloomingdale's. We even popped into Tiffany's on 5th Avenue. Rita then worked her magic on a couple of cops in Greenwich Village and asked for their recommendation of a 'must see' attraction. They recommended taking the Staten Island ferry across the bay to the island but, "Don't get off, there's nothing to see there. Just stay on the ferry for the return trip. You'll pass the Statue of Liberty and get the most amazing view of Manhattan as you come back." He was right.

By the time we left New York on Sunday, this time down the back on a 747, we felt that we had seen about as much as we could fit in over the weekend. However, the birthday was not yet over. We had a couple of tickets for the Monday evening, the actual day of her birthday, for Phantom of the Opera, up in London. Having parked the car, we were walking to the theatre when we heard, coming up from some basement steps, the sounds of a party. It was a club and a notice stuck on the door announced that it was a party celebrating an anniversary of the club's opening. Invited guests only. We knocked on the door and I explained that it was Rita's birthday. We were invited in and given champagne (on the House) and nibbles before we had to leave for the theatre. All in all, it turned out to be a truly memorable birthday.

BOMB ONBOARD

O n February 27th 1987 'XK', the British Airways 747, callsign 'Speedbird 282,' departed from LAX, Los Angeles International Airport, on the flight to London's Heathrow on a beautiful clear evening. The departure was the standard one, taking off to the west, out to sea and then, under radar control, a gentle turn to the left bringing the 'Speedbird' round to fly inbound towards the coast and crossing into California again to the south of Longbeach, where those passengers on the left of the aircraft would get a good view of the Queen Mary at its permanent anchor.

The captain was Jo and the flight engineer was Dave. Jo had given me, his co-pilot, the sector and so I was flying the aircraft whilst Jo was talking to Los Angeles on our departure radar frequency.

As we continued our climb towards our cruising altitude the route would take us over Las Vegas on its northerly track into Canada for its transatlantic crossing to the UK. The weather forecast for the whole route was good and we would be arriving into London slightly ahead of our scheduled time the following morning.

After the seat belt signs had been extinguished, the chief steward had come onto the flight deck to make his standard report to the captain that the evening meal was being prepared for the passengers and there were no problems in the cabin.

By the time we had reached our initial cruising altitude we were talking to Radar Control and about halfway between Los Angeles and Las Vegas.

The radar controller suddenly said, "Speedbird 282, call your company on Los Angeles company frequency. They have an urgent message for you."

Whilst it was not unusual to get messages from the company as we departed a station it rarely happened that they were classed as urgent. The flight engineer and I listened in as Jo called Speedbird Los Angeles. The message was not good.

"Speedbird 282, this is Speedbird Los Angeles. We have received a phone call specifying your flight as having a bomb on board. This was an unidentified call but was specific to your flight and we can therefore only treat it as genuine."

It is true to say that many airlines receive calls about explosive devices on board from time to time. Virtually all turn out to be hoaxes with the intention, presumably, of causing disruption for whatever personal reason the caller may have. Over time, airlines have had to develop a strategy to weed out the obvious hoaxes from the possible genuine calls but, when doubt remains, a call would carry more weight if it were specific to a flight.

There followed a discussion between Jo and the company as to what our actions would be, and it was decided that we would assume the worst and act accordingly. This meant landing at the nearest suitable airfield and evacuating the aircraft as swiftly as possible.

We were now about halfway between Los Angeles and Las Vegas and we decided that we would turn back to Los Angeles where we were familiar with the airport and we knew that the emergency services on the ground were first class.

We made the radar controller aware of our problem and requested an immediate return to Los Angeles. We were given radar vectors for the airport and a level for our initial descent.

Jo called the chief steward up onto the flight deck to make him aware of our situation and to brief him of our plans. He was told to brief the cabin crew discreetly and to make them aware that after landing and parking in a safe area we would be carrying out an emergency evacuation of all passengers and crew using all the inflatable slides available. He, or the other cabin crew, were not to tell any of the passengers the real situation in case there was any sort of panic.

Jo said, "I will talk to everybody on the P.A. and tell them that we are returning to Los Angeles because of a technical problem and ask for their forbearance and to follow the instructions of the crew. I will talk to them all again after landing and brief them on the emergency evacuation."

It was now quite dark outside but, being a clear night, the lights of greater Los Angeles area were shining very brightly. It occurred to me that if the device we possibly had onboard was sophisticated it may have been set to trigger by the barometric change of our pressure during a descent. I discussed this with Jo and Dave, the flight engineer, and said that I thought it might be a good idea to ask radar control if we might fly over the least densely populated area during our descent and approach to landing. If the aircraft were to explode it would be better if this occurred over open countryside than heavily populated areas.

With radar assistance we made our final approach and landing on one of the westerly runways. The tower at LAX were very aware of our situation and our intention to evacuate rapidly and directed us to a large, deserted concrete pan, well away from the busy traffic areas.

During the taxi to this area Jo briefed the passengers of our intentions and asked them to follow the instructions of the cabin crew to the letter.

We came to a halt, shut down the engines and within seconds heard the doors slamming open followed by the automatic slides at each door inflating for the evacuation.

It was a full aeroplane but within under two minutes the chief steward came on the flight deck to announce that all passengers had disembarked and were away from the aircraft.

"Good! Evacuate all remaining crew to a clear distance and we'll be following you!"

Leaving the flight deck to the nearest slide the empty cabin was eerily quiet as I leaped onto the evacuation slide for the ride to the ground. At a safe distance our passengers were gathering and waiting to be taken by airport busses away from the area.

As I approached a large group of passengers one of them, whom I recognised as a close neighbour from my village at home and who was always asking when he might get to fly with me, approached me laughing and pointing his finger at me.

"You!! I should have known you would get to chuck me off your flight."

Meanwhile, the crew were being separated from the passengers to be taken away for a debriefing and a team of bomb disposal experts were arriving, complete with sniffer dogs, to check the aircraft thoroughly for explosives. There were, of course, none, as we suspected, but you can never be sure.

As to the flight crew, we three were taken to a hotel and were individually interviewed by experts from the Federal Aviation Authority (FAA), going over each and every aspect of the flight and the decisions made, with the reasons for those decisions. Our flight licences were taken from us and would not be returned for a few days until the FAA were satisfied that everything was carried out according to recognised procedures.

TOWARDS COMMAND

I n BA we operated a 'bid-line' system. Each month's work would contain approximately the same amount of duty comprising one or more trips. The longer the trips the fewer there were in a month's work. Each crew member was provided, some weeks in advance, with a list of work 'lines' containing all the trips the fleet would fly for that month. You were invited to place a list of 'bids' for the work lines you would like to fly in order of preference. They would then be 'awarded' in order of seniority of the individuals. It follows, therefore, that if you were the most senior pilot on the fleet you would expect to get your first choice, and so on down the list of seniority. At the bottom of the list, you would get the dregs. Your quality of life depended very much upon your position on the list.

As a co-pilot you would expect to progress up the list as more senior co-pilots became captains and so life would become sweeter. However, command (captaincy) vacancies would only become available as captains retired and if, like me, you had joined the airline as a fairly elderly pilot (30 years old) there would be a great many pilots in front of you of a younger age.

However, eventually I was within sight of being able to apply for a command. If I had been prepared to move to Manchester, I would have been able to get a command flying short haul on the BA 1-11 a year or two earlier than I did but I wanted to remain at Heathrow. I wasn't up for moving house and disrupting either family any further. In the event by mid-1988 I applied for a command course on the Boeing 757. Whilst it was short haul flying it was based at Heathrow and I might have the option of transferring back to long-haul in the future.

The command course was at Cranebank, naturally, and consisted of the usual ground school lessons on all the aircraft systems. From day one I was teamed up with a co-pilot who was converting on to the aircraft and I was treated as the captain, sitting in the captain's left-hand seat. We sat in a mock-up of the 757 flight deck which everybody called 'the cardboard bomber'. It had all the appropriate levers and switches, but it was designed just to learn all the drills. It did this quite effectively and prepared us for the simulator. Eventually we flew the aeroplane on normal scheduled routes with a training captain acting as the co-pilot. There were several trips scheduled like this and when it was considered I was ready I was teamed up with the 757 Flight Manager for my 'command check'. My check was from Heathrow to Newcastle and back, a normal passenger service. All the decisions were mine, as 'captain' and, on returning to Heathrow the Flight Manager shook my hand and said, "Welcome to the fleet, Captain Warren. We'll programme you to fly your first trip in command tomorrow." It was a l..o..n..g time coming!

When I arrived home that night Rita and Tania were waiting in the drive bouncing up and down with excitement as I got out of the car with my captain's hat on.

The 757 was a very pleasant aeroplane to fly and was the smaller sibling of the 747 but, being newer, had a more sophisticated flight system. It was a two-pilot operation, and the route structure was just the UK and Europe.

I found, as I had suspected, that the shorter sectors and lack of intercontinental travel did not satisfy me the way the 747 had. I also preferred the longer time off between trips of the long-haul lifestyle rather than the very much more frequent trips to and from Heathrow that the 757 demanded. However, it was good to have command of my own aeroplane at last after eighteen years in BA.

In December of 1988 I asked Rita to marry me. She agreed and the next morning I contacted the local Registry Office in Beaconsfield and was told that the earliest date they could manage was Friday 13th January 1989: Five years to the day after we had met! Friday 13th was turning out to be a significant day for us.

We arranged a small-scale wedding at home with family and a few friends after which we flew off on our honeymoon to Cape Town.

I had not been on the 757 for more than fifteen months when the new Boeing 747-400 started to arrive in BA. This was the opportunity I had been waiting for. I asked Rita how she felt about my possibly applying for long-haul again. She said it was entirely my decision and she would live with whatever I decided.

My first sight of the new aircraft was when I found myself parked next to one at terminal 4. I was due to fly off to Amsterdam, but I had a few spare minutes when I could go over and investigate the flight deck. Wow! What a ship! It had that new car smell, and everything was shiny and new. I really had to have one. By the time I climbed back into my 757 it was like getting into a Skoda after sitting in a Rolls.

747-400

Whilst, under normal circumstances, the company would not be prepared to countenance giving me another expensive conversion course in less than five years, I knew that it took time for an aircraft to settle into its place in the airline before the more senior captains would be prepared to move to it. This was because, there being fewer of the aeroplanes when they first arrive, the routes would be quite restricted and unattractive for these senior guys. I applied and was accepted due to the lack of applicants. When I told Rita, she pumped the air with her fist and said, "Yess!"

By late 1989 therefore I found myself back at Cranebank on the 747-400 course. This aeroplane really was state-of-the-art. Whilst it looked like a slightly larger 747 with a stretched upper deck all the systems were new, and the flight deck looked a bit like the Star ship Enterprise. Gone were all the old analogue instruments and in came the latest flat-screen digital displays. The simulators in which we were going to spend many hours were also space-age technology. They were so realistic that it was now possible, and accepted by the CAA, for the crews to do virtually the whole conversion course in the simulator and not go near the aeroplane until they were ready to fly with passengers. In fact, what actually happened was that after the simulator course I flew with a training captain on the flight deck on a normal passenger service. Again, as with the 757, when it was Judged I was ready, I flew a 'route check' with a training captain after which the ship was mine.

For the first few months I found that I was picking up some quite decent trips. This, despite the fact that I was a very junior captain. As I suspected, lots of the senior guys were avoiding the 400 for the time being and I found myself fairly close to the top of the seniority list on the fleet. Of course, this would not last and, as the fleet attracted more pilots, I found myself progressively moving down the list. Still, the 400 didn't seem to have any bad trips, just less-good ones.

Within a few months we had the news we had been hoping for. The fleet was going to start Australian postings as per the old 747. Rita and I discussed her retiring from her job so that she could join me for the whole three-month tour in Sydney, should I be lucky enough to get one.

In January of 1991 I was accepted for a Sydney posting and Rita, now having retired, was able to come with me. Whilst she had been on several trips with me, both on the 757 and latterly on the 400, this was going to be three months in one of the world's most attractive cities.

On arrival in Sydney, we wasted no time in looking for an apartment in Manly, on the far side of Sydney harbour from the city. We found one on the seventh floor of a tower block right on the beach with views from the balcony along Ocean Beach. It was perfect for our needs and had two bedrooms just in case we had family visitors.

Getting to work was easy. From the apartment I could walk to the Manly ferry terminal where I would take the ferry across to Circular Quay, walk up the hill to the Intercontinental Hotel where the crew stayed and catch the crew transport to the airport. Coming back from service was the same in reverse, except that I could normally get the crew transport to drop me off at circular quay and save me the walk. This was a very pleasant way to spend three months flying.

Most of the flight crews on the posting were living either in Manly or, in some cases, had rented properties on the north shore to the north of Manly. This meant that the postings were very social, and we quite often met up with other crews or families, either in local restaurants or on Shelley Beach for a barbecue. When husbands were away flying, wives were always included in any get-togethers and some close friendships were forged.

Between trips there was sometimes sufficient time off to be able to go away on mini holidays and Rita and I took advantage of this to the full. We visited Malaysia and New Zealand not to mention most cities in Australia. Rita even took herself off to fly to Port Douglas, north of Cairns in Queensland where she snorkelled on the Great Barrier Reef.

During this posting Tania was living up on the Gold Coast where she was sharing a flat with a friend. We managed to see her and her Australian friends from time to time, either when she came down to Sydney or when we went up to the Gold Coast.

On each posting one of the BA captains is designated 'Base Captain' for the flight crews on the base. He deals with London directly to sort out any administration problems on the base and he keeps records of the crews work schedules and allowance claims put in by the pilots. One morning I was contacted by the base captain and asked if I would be prepared to appear on Australia's Channel 7 TV as a BA pilot to hand out a prize to a viewer which was connected with the release of the film 'Robin Hood'. The prize was a flight to London, hence BA, and a weekend in a hotel in Nottingham, near Sherwood Forest.

"It's no big deal," he said "It's just that you are the only captain on the base available on that day. You will need to turn up in full uniform and you will be on the 'Good Morning Australia' slot for a couple of minutes with the presenter Ann Sanders."

I agreed, and on the appointed day a car from the TV station turned up at our apartment block and took me to the studios. Rita came with me and there was a PR lady in the car with us briefing me on what it was all about.

"You will be called on for the last three or four minutes of the programme and there will be a large barrel on a stand, and you will wind the handle and pick out a winning name from the small trap door. That person will have won the prize donated by British Airways, whom you are representing."

"Will there be any questions to which I should know the answers?"

"No, Ann is a lovely lady, and she will introduce you and engage in some small talk about your job and then invite you to spin the barrel. The previous guest will be a round-the-world solo yachtsman. We'll call you on when we're ready."

At the studio Rita and I sat away at one side and watched the yachtsman telling Ann some horrendous stories about his boat capsizing in stormy seas and all the terrifying things you imagine could befall a lone sailor several hundred miles away from the nearest help. By the time I was called on to the set I was beginning to feel a little worried about what Ms. Sanders might ask me about flying.

"Next, we have the great honour to welcome on our programme one of British Airways senior captains to draw our prize. Captain Les Warren. Good morning Captain." I thought, but didn't say, "You have me because I was the only one available today."

"Captain, it must be a very exciting job you do to fly a 747 Jumbo."

"Well, Ann, not as exciting as your previous guest I'm pleased to say. Quite ordinary in comparison."

There then followed a few questions about what it was like to fly to Australia and how long it took, etc. etc.

Ann then got on with the business in hand, introducing the prize to be given away and, "The captain will now spin the barrel and pick out the winning name." I handed the slip of paper with the winning name on it to Ann who announced the winner and that was the first and last time I have ever appeared on TV.

Too soon the posting came to an end and we were back in London and I was on to normal route flying, without the Australian / New Zealand sectors. In fact, as the older 747 was being phased out and the company bought more 400's the route structure on the aircraft was expanding and we were picking up some quite attractive destinations. To service the extra flying the fleet required more crews and so, as more senior captains arrived, my name slipped slowly away from the top of the list and closer to the bottom and my work choices became less attractive. I would just have to keep an eye open for another posting.

This, in fact, happened sooner than I had expected. By February 1992 I was awarded a further Sydney posting and Rita and I soon found ourselves flat hunting in Manly once more. This time we found a really special, brand-new apartment, right on the beach on Ocean Beach side of Manly. It was on the first floor and had a large balcony looking, unobstructed, out to sea.

Having so recently completed a posting we were soon 'back in the saddle' and planning our off-duty time visiting places we had missed out before. We couldn't believe our luck that we had managed to miss the best part of two consecutive winters in the UK.

On one trip flying down from Bangkok to Sydney I noticed from the air a beautiful looking island off the north east coast of Malaysia. I looked at our navigation readout to see the co-ordinates of the island so that I could identify it at a travel agency after I landed. It turned out to be Perhentian and Rita and I organised a trip there from Australia in my time off. It was not easy to reach and entailed a flight from Kuala Lumpur, a long taxi ride and then a long boat trip, but it was worth it. It was quite undeveloped but had beautiful beaches and stunning coral reefs just off the beach.

This time I managed to go with Rita up to Port Douglas to take a cruise out to the Barrier Reef. It was quite spectacular. The clarity of the water and the colours of the fish amongst the reef were indescribable.

By the time we had finished this posting we heard on the grapevine that BA were considering finishing with the base in Sydney for various reasons but mainly on cost I should imagine. The 400 was probably turning out to be more reliable than they had imagined and therefore having a pool of crews in Sydney to be called upon in the event of disruptions wasn't really cost effective. For whatever reason I was determined to achieve one more posting if at all possible. I was lucky enough to go out to Sydney for one last time in December of 1992 for a final three month posting. This time I was asked to take the position of Base Captain which meant that I was given a fax machine which spewed out yards of paper every night with information about BA's operations whether we wanted it or not.

I don't know how we did it, but we managed to rent the same apartment we had on our previous posting, right on the beach at Manly. The other residents in the block believed that we were the owners and would be coming out each year. It was rather comforting to see the same familiar faces.

The useful thing about being in Manly was that we didn't have to have a car. Everywhere was within walking distance and the city was only a ferry ride away across what must be one of the most beautiful harbours in the world. On the rare occasions we found we needed wheels, the taxis were plentiful and reasonably priced.

BA had one very popular flight from Auckland in New Zealand to Perth, Western Australia and then on to London. A posting crew would fly from Sydney to Auckland and then from Auckland to Perth where they would hand over to another crew to take the aircraft on to Singapore. The sector between Auckland and Perth was invariably full. There was some sort of a deal with the tickets which ensured its popularity.

On this occasion I was the captain out of Auckland, but I had handed the sector over to my co-pilot, giving him responsibility for all the decisions. As with most BA flights at that time we welcomed passengers on to the flight deck by special invitation but in limited numbers. After I made the initial introduction on the PA, I handed over all other PA announcements to the co-pilot. I did, however, listen in to his PA.

We had not been airborne very long when the co-pilot said that we welcomed anybody on to the flight deck. I said, "Well mate, you'll be sorry! You invited them so you can speak to them – all of them."

Seconds later the chief steward burst through the flight deck door and said, "Well thank you! We have started the meal service and four hundred passengers stood up and tried to make their way up to the flight deck! What would you like me to tell them?"

For the next two hours or so we were treated to a stream of passengers pushing their way through the door and firing the *same* questions at the co-pilot. Not me, because I was pointedly looking out of the window watching the clouds roll by.

FINAL YEARS

I n BA at that time, pilots had to retire on their 55th birthday. This rule had been in place for many years and reflected the thinking in the post-war period when it was assumed that a 55-year-old was, well, old. This rule was to change a short time after I reached 55! (was this a co-incidence?) It was interesting that most other airlines had a retirement age of 60 for its pilots, and in some cases, 65. For this reason, it was not uncommon for retired BA pilots to join other airlines for a few years after leaving BA. In this way other airlines must have saved millions in training costs thanks to BA's short-sighted view.

After my last posting I was in the last three years of service with BA. The routes for the 400 had improved as we picked up newer destinations and I was pleased to take advantage of flying to countries I had never visited before. I had my first visits to South America flying to Rio, Sao Paulo, Buenos Aires, and Santiago. I even managed to take Rita with me to all except Santiago, where it was just a transit stop. It was lovely to share my travels with her.

Now, years after I had left Zambia whilst in the RAF, I was scheduled to take a service to Lusaka, the capital of Zambia. I was determined that Rita should come with me as we would have a couple of days off and I might be able to arrange an interesting trip.

On arrival in Lusaka, I contacted the Air Headquarters of the Zambia Air Force and was amazed to find that the man in charge, the Air Commander, was General Shikapwasha, one of my old students from Livingstone in the mid 60's. I was put through to him on the telephone and he said he would be delighted to meet up. I told him that I remembered when I was in the ZAF that there used to be a shuttle aircraft that flew between Lusaka and Livingstone and, if it was still operating, was there any chance that Rita and I could get a ride to Livingstone so I could show her the sights? He promised to look into it.

Later, in our hotel, a message was passed to me at the front desk saying that a ZAF car would pick us up early the next morning to take us out to the ZAF base at the International Airport.

Sure enough, the next morning we met a smartly dressed gentleman in the lobby waiting to take us out to the base. He would be looking after us for the day and would accompany us down to Livingstone in their twin-engine turboprop aircraft.

When we arrived at the steps of the aircraft, which was a Chinese twelve passenger seat model I had never seen before, I was embarrassed to discover that Rita and I plus our PR man were the only passengers on the flight. I asked if it was unusual for the shuttle to have so few passengers.

"No, Bwana," he said, "We don't have a shuttle anymore. This flight is for you only as the guest of the Zambia Air Force."

I was quite taken aback. I knew that the Zambian economy was struggling and yet they had laid on this aircraft especially for me with its two pilots.

As we approached Livingstone, I could see the familiar spray from the Falls and the PR man said that we would fly around the Falls so that we could get a good view. It was as spectacular as I remembered it from some thirty years before and I was so pleased that I could share it with Rita.

After landing we were met on the aircraft apron by the ZAF Livingstone Station Commander. He introduced himself along with his other senior staff and told us that his official car and driver would be at our disposal for the whole day to go wherever we wanted. I just had not expected this. If we had just flown back to Lusaka there and then we would have had a brilliant experience, but I was speechless at this great honour. It would also seem that the two pilots would just wait by their aircraft until we returned.

Of course, we thanked the Station Commander profusely and asked him if it would be in order for us to drive to the Falls to see it at close quarters. "Naturally," he said, "Anything you would like, but if you could be back here by about 4pm that would be perfect."

We had a wonderful day. The Falls at that time of year were in full flood and we had a good soaking from the spray. When we had seen the thundering Zambesi crashing into the gorges beneath from every conceivable viewpoint, we made our bedraggled way back to the car. I asked if we could take a drive along 'Riverside Drive' for old-times' sake as far as I was concerned so that I could show Rita where we used to spend a great deal of our time. We were also able to drive through the Livingstone Game Park to see some of the game in the area. It was a pity that we wouldn't see any elephants as, at that time of year with water plentiful, they would not be coming down to the river.

On the way back to the airfield we drove through the town and I was able to show Rita where I lived. I was quite surprised to find that not a great deal had changed over the years, but I imagine that there had not been a great deal to attract investors.

On the flight back to Lusaka we were told that the pilot was going to land at what used to be the old airport on the edge of the town so that we were close to our hotel. He would then fly back to the ZAF base at the international airport where he picked us up that morning. It appeared that they just could not do enough for us. However, there was more to come. On arrival we were met by a colonel who handed us an invitation to dinner that evening as guests of the Air Commander at a local restaurant. General Shikapwasha and several senior officers with their wives would be present. Of course, we accepted, and were told that the official car would pick us up later that evening from our hotel.

Neither of us travels on these trips with a formal evening dress and Rita was beside herself thinking that our hosts would dress for the occasion and we would have to 'make-do' with what we had. Maybe the lighting in the restaurant would be dim.

Our worst fears were realised when, on arrival, we saw that the officers were in their smart best uniforms and their ladies were in Zambian national dress. I'm sure we looked OK, but that's as far as I would go.

It was good to see 'Shikap' again, as I used to call him, but this evening I called him General! There were a couple of other officers there who I was told were just about joining the Flying Training School as the RAF were leaving but I couldn't honestly say I remembered them. I mentioned some names and were told of their fortunes, good and bad, and all in all we had a lovely meal in good company.

At the end of the evening Shikap stood up and made a speech by way of welcoming us and then, to our great embarrassment, made us a presentation of a set of copper goblets and a copper animal picture which you could buy from the vendors selling their wares at the Victoria Falls. Copper was a locally mined commodity in Zambia and was hard to avoid. Rita and I avoided looking at each other as I stood up to make my reply because, just a few weeks before this trip, we had taken all our copper ornaments from my time in Zambia, which we both disliked anyway, down to the local charity shop in Thame. I had to try to appear overwhelmed, which in a way, I was!

On the way back to our hotel we agreed that we would have to put our new gifts up in the loft at home but somewhere we could find it in a hurry in case we had visitors from the ZAF.

TEHERAN

With just a year to go I had one unforgettable trip.

It was a night departure from New Delhi, and we had virtually a full aircraft, about 400 passengers and a considerable amount of freight including several pallets of fresh fruit and vegetables. We were flying direct to London's Heathrow airport and, because of the length of flight we were carrying an extra co-pilot. This was quite standard on the Boeing 747-400, although the normal operating complement of flight deck crew was two pilots, a captain and a co-pilot, the operating sectors were usually sufficiently long that the rules required an extra pilot to allow one pilot at a time to take a sleeping rest. At the back of the flight deck there was a bunk rest room with two bunks. On ultra-long haul sectors, a complete extra crew was carried, another captain and co-pilot. On this night we had just the one extra co-pilot, one of BA's first female pilots.

We started off with the normal two pilots and Mandy, our extra co-pilot, took the first rest and went into the bedroom shortly after take-off. The plan was that by the time we reached London each of the pilots would have had a substantial rest, effectively allowing us to extend the normal flight time limitations. The route would take us north west flying over Afghanistan and then Iran and into Europe and would be in the dark most of the way until an early morning arrival into LHR. Having left Indian airspace, the route was relatively quiet, and the night was very clear as we entered into Iranian airspace at around 35,000 feet. The co-pilot, Mike, and I were chatting whilst the stars glistened above us and below there was just one dark void with no sign of life.

At a time like this the flight deck is a very peaceful place with the glow of the instrument lights and the usual flight noises from working equipment and airflow over the cockpit. Suddenly we were violently alerted by the loud 'Fire Warning' bell and the bright red fire warning light above our heads. It indicated a fire in the hold where the freight and passenger bags were stored. At a time like this the first action is for the pilot, in this case me, to pull out the emergency check list and, along with the co-pilot, work our way through all the items associated with that particular emergency. We knew that there was no way physically to check in the hold in flight as there was no access from inside the aircraft and so our only indication was the warning system which is basically a smoke alarm. If the sensors detect smoke or any interference of the light beam in the sensors, then the fire warning is triggered. In the past there had been a few spurious warnings of fire when fruit and vegetables had been carried due to vapour being given off from this freight which the smoke alarms had interpreted as smoke, and thus fire. We had no way of telling which we had so we had to plan for the worst-case scenario and hope for the best.

As soon as I picked up the checklist the warning stopped, and the fire warning light extinguished. Mike and I looked at each other and we each breathed a sigh of relief as I returned the checklist to its stowage. As soon as I did that, the warning blared out again. I picked up the checklist again, opened it and, action replay, light out, warning bell off.

"OK, Mike", I said, "Next time we do the full drill regardless", hoping against hope that there would not be a next time. The next time happened almost straight away so we went straight into the drill.

We had to plan to land at the nearest suitable airfield, which in this case was Teheran. Immediately I could see a possible problem here as we had a few Israeli passengers and things could get difficult on the ground. As captain I had a responsibility to all my passengers but first we had to get safely on the ground. We had two fire extinguishers in the hold area which we would activate from the flight deck and, hopefully, if there was a fire it would be extinguished. We also had to stop any flow of air into the hold so as not to feed the fire. Landing early in the flight meant that we had a lot of fuel on board and we would have to jettison a good deal of this to get us down to an acceptable landing weight. Jettisoned fuel leaves the aircraft from discharge pipes at the wingtips and comes out at about two tons per minute in two long streams. Any passenger looking out of the window could well be quite alarmed by this, so I would have to wake them up and explain what we were doing. I called the Head of Cabin Crew up to the flight deck and explained the situation and our intention to land in Teheran. I told him I was about to speak to the passengers, but he would undoubtedly have to field a lot of questions and he needed to have the crew prepare for a possible emergency landing but to take no action until my announcement. On the PA system I told the passengers that,

"We are starting our descent into Teheran because we have a technical issue which will need to be sorted out by our staff on the ground. During the descent we will be getting rid of some of our fuel as we need to reduce the weight for landing and so you may see streams of fuel flowing out of the wingtips – this is quite normal. We will also be adjusting the air pressure in the cabin and so you may experience some pressure changes on your ears. I'll be making a perfectly normal landing in about ten minutes and so I will speak to you again after we stop. Meanwhile my cabin crew will go about their duties preparing for our arrival in Teheran."

On our descent towards Teheran, we would have to slowly decrease the pressurisation to stop the possibility of airflow into the hold feeding the fire. Next, I needed to talk to

Teheran, where it was about 2am, and explain that we were making an unscheduled emergency landing at their airfield and I would explain what I would require of them when they were ready to copy. Meanwhile, we decided that it might be a good idea to wake Mandy up in the bunk with a bell we have on the flight deck which sounds in the bedroom. We must have pressed the bell 3 or 4 times before there was any sign of Mandy who had obviously been fast asleep. She opened the bedroom door and, on her knees said, "OK, OK, where's the F......g fire!" "In the hold!" we shouted, "Get dressed!"

The man in the tower at Teheran seemed a little confused as to why we were coming to his airfield, so I had to spell it out. I told him to alert our British Airways staff at the airfield for their full assistance. I told him that we had a possible fire in the hold and that we would need to evacuate the passengers as quickly as possible from all the doors on the port side of the aircraft. This was because the doors to the holds were on the starboard side and I wanted the fire services on that side. Because we had 400 or so passengers, we would need a lot of buses on that port side and steps up to each door as soon as we stopped. Further, on landing I would need fire engines to be stationed about halfway down the runway and to follow the aircraft in its final run towards the end of the runway and inform me straightaway if there was any sign of fire from the area of the holds. I would want to leave the runway as soon as my speed allowed and wanted to stop at the first convenient place rather than taxy for miles with a possible fire on board. If there was fire, I would need to evacuate the passengers down the emergency slides on the port side only and we would brief the passengers to get away from the aircraft as soon as they were on the ground. Nobody but nobody was to open the holds until all the passengers and crew were out of the aircraft. This was because the sudden flow of oxygen to the fire, if there was one, would have disastrous consequences.

Our arrival was a bit like the Keystone Cops. On touchdown I noticed that the fire engines were by the touchdown point and, unless they could drive at about 110 knots, they would not be anywhere near me when I turned off the runway. So, I turned off the runway with the fire engines in the distance, trundling towards us and, although there were buses in our vicinity they seemed to be very reluctant to approach us so I shut down the engines and had the cabin crew prepare to disembark the passengers. I explained on the PA that they would be disembarking and would be taken by the buses to the terminal building whilst we sorted out the technical problem.

Once the steps were at the aircraft and the doors were opened our Teheran BA representative came onto the flight deck and we discussed the problem. The passengers meanwhile were disembarking into the buses and taken to the terminal lounges on the airside. I told our rep. that I wanted the passengers to stay airside as I did not want them to go through the Iranian arrival procedure as we hoped to leave Teheran as soon as we had the problem sorted. When the head of cabin crew reported that all passengers were off the aeroplane the remaining crew disembarked and I went downstairs to the starboard side by the freight doors and gave instructions that the hold doors should be opened slowly with the fire engines ready in case there were flames. There were no flames! However, the hold had to be emptied completely as it was possible something may have been smouldering. As soon as I saw the pallets of fruit and vegetables, I knew we had the source of our 'fire'.

I had to check in our operating manuals whether the aircraft could be flown with no fire suppressant system fitted (we had emptied both extinguisher bottles on descent and there were no replacements in Teheran). The answer was, yes, but the hold had to be completely empty so that meant leaving all the freight and the passengers' luggage in Teheran to be flown to London by somebody else. All we had to do now was to have BA in London produce another flight plan for us at our new weight (no freight) with the fuel we would need for LHR. We would then need to get the aircraft refuelled and prepared for departure. The one thing I did know was that, if there was a list of priority departures from Teheran, we would be at the bottom of it. We were off schedule and therefore didn't feature in Iranian plans. However, the really pressing issue was one of crew duty times. We knew that the latest time for our arrival into LHR would be based upon our departure time from Delhi and we had little time to play with. We really had to work something out. I knew that I had the discretion, as captain, to extend the duty time of each flight crew member by half the time that each of us had undisturbed time in the bunk. That meant that we could extend by one and a half hours if we each had three hours in the bunk. I could say that I would go into the bunk immediately after departure from Teheran for three hours followed by Mike for his three hours. Mandy's time didn't matter. She would make up the second operating pilot and she had already had her rest. With a bit of sharp pencilling, we would have to leave Teheran within the next hour or so if we wanted to avoid a report having to be filed to the CAA and the subsequent letter of complaint to BA.

We were getting dangerously close to the time when we would not be able to make London, even with our duty time extended to the maximum, and I would have to make a decision to a) Return to Delhi, or b) Divert to another airport, possibly in the middle east, or c) Divert into an airport in Europe if we could legally get that far. At this point my preference was c). I knew that, of the 400 passengers onboard, not one of them would want to return to Delhi but I would make my decision once we were airborne and we knew what our options were. For the time being I would honestly be able to tell the passengers that we were heading 'towards' London and update them when we were approaching our destination, wherever that may be.

Time was marching on and I needed to go and speak to the passengers, who by this time had spent a couple of hours in the departure lounge near the boarding gate and would be getting very anxious. Our rep took me across to the lounge (where there had been very little refreshment and some tempers were getting a little frayed). I had to stand on a chair to make myself visible and speak through a loud hailer. I explained that we would be re-boarding them all as soon as the aircraft was ready, and we would be taking them towards London. I then had to explain that we would not be taking their bags from the hold and why this would be so but that we fully expected them to arrive in London by another aircraft in the near future. I then found myself besieged by passengers who wanted me to know why they shouldn't be in Teheran, or why they needed to be in London, or how they needed to attend a wedding that very day and so on. I had to walk away telling my followers that I needed to prepare the aircraft for departure and feeling a bit like the Prime Minister leaving number ten and having questions fired at him by the press.

The new flight plan had arrived from BA in London, the aeroplane was refuelled and so we needed the passengers aboard. This took quite a while as by now the airport at Teheran was beginning to wake up for its early morning departures and we were not a priority. Everything was a bit like trying to run through treacle but eventually we were all buttoned up and ready to go and awaiting a clearance from Teheran Air Traffic Control to start our engines for departure.

Once in the air and safely on our way we knew we could not legally make London but Frankfurt, in Germany where BA had a good presence, was within our crew time limitations. I therefore changed our flight plan destination and alerted BA that we would be arriving in Frankfurt with 400 people who wanted to be in London and had no luggage. Our crew would be out of duty time and would therefore need to go to a hotel in Frankfurt and BA would have to arrange for a new crew to take the aeroplane on to London or make other arrangements for the passengers. I would only tell the passengers about the new plan just before our descent into Frankfurt when I might have some news from BA in London as to their onward journey. There was nothing to be gained by telling them anything now. It was also entirely possible that London was not necessarily the final destination for some of the passengers who might want to fly to other destinations which could easily be reached from Frankfurt.

Like all of these situations I had a responsibility to make sure the passengers were safe, and the aircraft was operated in accordance with this. I felt that we had handled the aircraft as demanded by the circumstances and, with the options in front of us, had made the best decisions for the good of the passengers. I can't think of anything I would have done differently but we did have one other option which I have not mentioned. We could have had the passengers, and the crew, proceed through the arrival procedure at Teheran and be taken to hotels by BA. My main reason for rejecting this idea was that we had a few Israeli passengers on board and there may have been some problems with the Iranians because of this and also because it seemed preferable to get the passengers as close to their destination in the shortest time. By staying airside, we also avoided having to pass through Iranian immigration both on arrival and then on departure.

FAREWELL

With a few months to go before leaving the company BA would give you the option of providing you with a 'retirement trip' of your choice. This was not universally popular amongst the more senior of our colleagues as it meant that the company was effectively 'giving away' a trip to a more junior captain that might otherwise have been taken by the senior pilot when he made his choices. This was the reason that BA gave you a few months' notice so they could work around this problem.

My retirement trip was awarded to me about two months before I was due to leave. I had asked for Cape Town where we would have a few days off and I intended to take Rita with me.

It was a lovely trip. The weather was beautiful and the scenery, as usual, stunning. Cape Town was, after all, where Rita and I spent our honeymoon and so it was full of precious memories.

On departure I was taxiing out towards our take-off runway and made my usual personal introduction and welcoming announcement with brief details of the flight. After we were in the air and climbing away, our Head of Cabin Crew came onto the flight deck and said,

"There's an elderly gentleman and his wife onboard and he wants to know if you are the Les Warren who was at King Edward's School in Wakefield House and joined the RAF, because, if you are, he is your old English Master. Guy's name is Bertie Mawer."

"Good grief, yes, I am. Please ask him to come up to see us when he is able."

Bertie came on to the flight deck with Rosemary, his wife, and we spent a very pleasant hour or so talking over old times. It was just incredible to think that after all these years he was still involved with King Edward's School. Meanwhile, I had left the school and had a full career flying, first in the RAF and now in the airline, and we meet again on my retirement trip.

Before he left the flight deck, I asked him if he would like to come up again before we started our descent into Heathrow and to stay with us for the approach and landing. I told him I would get a member of the crew to bring him up at the appropriate time.

At the top of descent Bertie came back up and we settled him into the spare crew seat behind me. For anybody who has not experienced the procedure of arrival into one of the world's busiest airports it is fascinating. The approach to Heathrow is strictly controlled through its various phases by a series of controllers using radar, with one controller handing you over to the next, handling not just ourselves but a series of arriving aircraft through his or her sector. If the sector is busy you may be required to enter a holding pattern over a particular radio beacon depending upon your arrival sector. Each aircraft in 'the hold', will fly a published racetrack pattern around the beacon, one of a series set around Heathrow. These aircraft are separated by height and the first to arrive in the pattern will be the lowest with each subsequent arriving aircraft positioned above the earlier flight. When the lowest aircraft is 'picked off' by radar to commence an approach, the other aircraft in the holding pattern each descend one level to take the place of the aircraft immediately beneath them.

Once you leave the hold, your radar controller hands you over to 'Approach Control' on a different radio frequency. The approach controller now positions you on the approach to the landing runway, separated from the other aircraft he is handling by about two minutes. During this phase you will be preparing the aircraft for its landing configuration with the lowering of flaps and the gear (wheels) and reducing the speed for touchdown.

If the weather is good there will be a good view of London, the Thames and all the familiar sights depending on your direction of approach. From the east you will see the Dome, Tower Bridge, and many other familiar sights, albeit from an unfamiliar aspect. From the west you may catch a glimpse of Windsor castle.

Once settled into a steady approach to the runway you will be further handed over to the controller in the tower who will clear you for the landing and monitor your flight until after touchdown, the roll along the runway, and turn off at the indicated point for taxying. Having left the runway, you will be handed over to the ground controller who will give you instructions for the route you will be taking to your parking bay, all the while you are carrying out your after landing procedures.

Once we were on our way to the terminal, I asked for a member of the cabin crew to take Bertie back to his seat and hoped that he had a memorable experience. I know that I did. It was a great privilege for me to be able to show Bertie how we handled things.

This wasn't actually my final trip as it had been awarded to me a couple of months before I left BA, but I had a few more trips to fly, none of which were particularly memorable which is, I suppose, a good thing. However, in my last couple of weeks I was asked if I would be interested in staying on for six months or so to fly as a co-pilot (three rings on my sleeve as opposed to the captains' four) being paid at the appropriate grade for a Senior First Officer, and also, of course, being paid my pension at the same time. It would appear that BA, at that time, were a little short of First Officers. I had no other pressing engagements and so I agreed. It did mean that I had to go back to the simulator to learn how to fly the aeroplane from the right-hand seat!

In practice it was an interesting situation. Whenever a member of the cabin crew came on to the flight deck and said, "Excuse me, Captain." I found that I would automatically turn round to answer. I also felt that some of the captains I flew with were a little uneasy, feeling perhaps, that I might be casting a critical eye over the way they were handling a situation. It wasn't at all unusual for a captain who, obviously, would be younger than me, to ask, "What do you think?" I might think, but not say, "Don't ask me, mate, I'm not paid to make those decisions!"

By and large though it worked well. I did manage to fly a trip to Beijing where I hadn't been before and, again, took Rita with me. We did all the compulsory sights including the Great Wall and the Forbidden City. We were overawed by the sheer magnitude of Tiananmen Square. We would probably never have done this if I had not stayed on as First Officer.

EXTRACURRICULAR

Some years before I retired from BA I had volunteered to go back to the RAF as a reserve officer where, during my free time between trips with the airline, I would fly Air Training Corps cadets in RAF Chipmunks to give the cadets air experience. Of course, I had a terrific amount of experience flying the chipmunk as I had instructed on it for many years. This was an unpaid position with the exception that the RAF would pay a fuel allowance to get you to the airfield. The big plus was that the ATC cadets would get to do some flying from time to time which might fire up their enthusiasm for aviation. It is probably true to say that most RAF pilots started out as Air Cadets.

Typically, a cadet would fly for perhaps thirty minutes during which time he or she could ask to do whatever they liked provided it was legal. Almost invariably they would ask to fly some aerobatics. As I used to enjoy aerobatics this was fine by me. Mind you, at the end of the day when you might have flown with nine cadets, if each had asked for aerobatics, you might be feeling a little jaded. Invariably I would allow each cadet to handle the aeroplane and give him or her a small amount of instruction. This generally went down very well, and they would feel that they had achieved something and would be keen to fly again.

When a group of cadets arrived at the AEF (Air Experience Flight) they would have to attend a briefing covering the things they might expect during their flight. This would be in the form of a film which would cover the whole flight profile, including the action to be taken should it be necessary to abandon the aeroplane in flight and how their pilot would initiate this for them. The film was at pains to point out that this was a very unlikely scenario, but they all needed to be aware of how to operate their parachute. At the end of the briefing, they were invited to ask questions and, after this, were taken to the flight hut where the first of the cadets would be fitted with flight overalls and strapped into their parachutes. They would then be shown how to deploy the parachute in an emergency and how to release themselves from the harness after landing.

In the flight hut the cadets would sit on chairs in a row (It was difficult to stand upright in a properly fastened parachute harness as the straps needed to be tight). They would wait for their pilots to arrive to take them out to the aircraft.

I would ask their names and would chat to them on the walk out to the aeroplane to try to make them feel at ease: some might feel a little apprehensive, especially if it were their first flight. I remember one occasion when the little lad (we'll call him Jimmy) who was to be my passenger was very subdued and obviously nervous. I tried to engage him in cheerful banter but to no effect. I really wanted him to enjoy his experience when he suddenly said,

"Sir, may I ask you a question?"

"Of course you may, Jimmy, anything you like."

"Well Sir, do I *have* to jump out when we're in the air?"

I did not know whether to laugh or cry. The poor kid was terrified, and he had fastened on the instructions in the film of jumping over the side of the aeroplane and using the parachute and had completely missed the "In the unlikely event, in the case of an emergency" part. I stopped, looked him in the eye and grasping both of his arms said,

"Jimmy, we will not be jumping out until we have finished our flight and we are back on the ground here and you have had a really exciting time, so let's go and get into the air."

His grin from ear to ear said it all!

Throughout the country there were several Air Experience Flights set up to serve ATC cadets and they were staffed by retired RAF pilots and, sometimes, currently serving pilots. The standards required of the pilots were up to normal RAF requirements and each pilot was regularly checked throughout the year by the Commanding Officer of the Flight. When I first applied to join an AEF, it was flying from Hurn airport which had, as its catchment area, ATC's from the south and south western counties. I was only able to do this for about three years as I then transferred to the 757 in BA for my command course and the drive down to Bournemouth did not fit in with my new flight schedules. Basically, I retired from the RAF Reserve but promised I would re-apply after retiring from BA.

With all my flying finished with BA I re-joined my old AEF which had now moved to Boscombe Down, near Amesbury. This was more convenient for me anyway as we were now living near Oxford, but it was still quite a long drive. The Chipmunk had now been replaced by the Bulldog, a more powerful propeller aircraft with side-by-side seating which was much better for the personal touch with cadets.

The countryside around Boscombe Down was a very interesting area to fly over. Shortly after take-off you would fly past Stonehenge and get a splendid bird's eye view of the site.

I was surprised at how many cadets had never heard of Stonehenge! What do they teach them at school these days? Our local flying area over which we could do aerobatics had Salisbury cathedral at one corner and the hills to the west of Salisbury had the various army regimental badges cut in the chalk on the hillsides – plenty for the cadets to see.

With a good flying day, it was possible for each AEF pilot to fly nine cadets. The first cadet would walk out to the aeroplane

with his pilot, be strapped in by a member of the groundcrew, and then the pilot would start up and taxi out for the flight. On return from the flight, the pilot would keep the engine running whilst a member of the groundcrew would unstrap the cadet and replace him or her with another cadet, all this whilst the pilot remained strapped in. In this way a quick changeover of cadets was possible with minimum loss of time.

The aim, of course, was to fly all the cadets who had arrived for the day. Nothing was more disappointing for a cadet than to miss out on a flight. Unfortunately, some ATC squadrons would turn up quite infrequently at their local AEF, for whatever reason, and so the trip that some cadets flew could turn out to be their only one whilst a member of their squadron.

A year or so into my retirement from BA I was finding that the drive to Boscombe Down was taking rather longer than I wanted. I had also discovered that, just a few miles away from our house, at RAF Benson, there was another AEF dealing with a different catchment area than the one at Boscombe Down. AEF pilots were always recruited locally by the Commanding Officer of the Flight who was generally a regular RAF officer. He would take into consideration not only the suitability of a prospective pilot but how available he might be based on his distance from the airfield. As I lived only about three miles away, I reckoned I stood a good chance, if he had any vacancies.

I paid him a visit at Benson, and he was quite keen to take me on. He liked the idea that he could get me to the airfield in less than half an hour with a quick phone call. It was now just a case of transferring, with the agreement of both CO's, from my old AEF at Boscombe Down, to the new one at Benson.

It all went seamlessly, and I was soon flying for my new AEF.

Whilst I was at Benson, the RAF decided that the Bulldog, which we were flying, was becoming a little 'long-in-the-tooth' and that we would be taking delivery of a new type of trainer, the Grob, manufactured in Germany and that it would be designated the 'Tutor T1'. Our first of the Tutors arrived in the new millennium and we soon appreciated its value. Like the Bulldog, it had side-by-side seating with, unusually, the captain sitting in the right-hand seat. The aeroplane was lighter, more economical, and very manoeuvrable making aerobatics a pleasure.

At about the same time that the new aircraft arrived we moved from our house in Oxfordshire to an apartment in Surrey, near Woking. I was now back to square one as far as travelling distance was concerned but I decided that I would have to stick with it. I could hardly swap AEF's again! In truth, I would have been closer to Boscombe Down, but why would they take me back? The difference in distance was marginal but the route from Woking to Benson was more tortuous.

By 2002 Rita and I had decided that we would move to Cyprus. We had been thinking about it for some time and had already paid the island a visit to get the feel of the place. It seemed to be what we wanted, and we found a small house as a temporary measure until we found something that we really would like.

During this time, I was able to fly back to the UK, where we still had a home, and drive to Benson for my AEF flying. If I thought that driving between Woking and Benson was a drag, then feeding in the flight from Cyprus on top of it made it extremely difficult. In truth, I could stay in the UK for a few days and do as much flying as possible so that the AEF could get maximum value from me, but I could see that this would not be a long-term solution.

The previous year I had passed my sixtieth birthday, and this was getting towards the age at which the RAF would be considering asking me to retire from flying for the AEF.

By 2003 therefore, I decided that I had really come to the end of the road and I would hang up my flying overalls. I spoke to the boss to tell him of my decision and he was flattering enough to try to persuade me to stay. One big problem was that, if a pilot had not flown for a month, he had to have a full flight check with the C.O. This effectively meant that each time I came in to fly I was having to have a check with the boss first, wasting time and resources, as I could not, in fairness, come back from Cyprus more than once a month. Even that was stretching it.

So, here we are at last. In a career that started in 1958 on a whim and the carrot of having three days off school, I have finally called it a day 45 years later. It is difficult to imagine how life could have been any better.

On my journey I have met aviators who have been desperate to hang on to the life of flying, looking to stay in the air, frightened to come down to earth. A bit like the ageing pop star we all pity, who no longer has it, but tries to live through his past glories, but that's not for me.

One of the advantages of a life in flying is that, although you have to spend some fairly lengthy periods of time away from home to the detriment of family life, you also find yourself in between trips spending very usable chunks of time at home. It is during these 'down' times that you find you can hone your DIY skills and take on jobs in the house or garden which normally employed individuals haven't the time to tackle. This, combined with the fact that retirement came early in the airline world of my day, gave me time to work on satisfying projects such as completely changing the inside layout of our house and then, after moving to a new house, designing, and building a new garden on a steep sloping site. Of course, I couldn't realistically have done this without the considerable planning skills of my wife, Rita, not to mention her willingness to muck in with the manual labour tasks. She is also a very knowledgeable gardener.

Sometimes, now, I look up into the sky when I see an aircraft passing overhead, more out of curiosity than of any longing. People with me have often said, "Bet you wish you were up there now." But, no, I don't. I have extracted a lot from my life in flying, perhaps more than I deserve. I have had some very good times and met some very kind and able people, sadly, many of whom are no longer with us. There have been a few, very few, scary moments but, on balance, flying has been good to me and I have had my share of luck and good fortune and I finally walk away from it with gratitude.

MT

Tel. No.

HOLBORN 3434, Ext.....................

Telegrams:
  Airministry London Telex
  Telex: 2-2406

Correspondence on the subject of this
letter should be addressed to:

THE UNDER-SECRETARY OF STATE,

AIR MINISTRY.........................

and should quote the reference:
A.255489/56/M.1a

Your Ref. ....

AIR MINISTRY,

ADASTRAL HOUSE,

THEOBALDS ROAD,

LONDON, W.C.1

16th September, 1958

Dear Sir,

      Final arrangements have now been made for your entry into training on a twelve year Direct Commission as a pilot in the General Duties Branch of the Royal Air Force on Thursday, 25th September, 1958.

2.   You should therefore proceed to No.1 Initial Training School South Cerney, Gloucestershire, on that date and joining instructions and a travel warrant for your journey to Cirencester are enclosed.

3.   May I take this opportunity of wishing you every success during your service in the Royal Air Force.

                      Yours faithfully,

                    Director of Manning

L.C. Warren, Esq.,
    24, Claremont Road,
      Hextable,
        Swanley,
          Kent.

Acceptance Letter to Join R.A.F.

Officer Cadets - 1 ITS 1958

Les - front right

On the flight line - 1959 Ternhill

Les after 1st solo - 16th March 1959, Ternhill

Bob Weetman and Les - Waiting for a Flight - Ternhill 1959

New Acting Pilot Officers of 148 Course, 6FTS, Ternhill, 1959
Les 3rd from left, front row

Provost T1 Taxying in at Ternhill 1959

Les in Vampire T.11 - 1960 Oakington

Vampire Formation Aerobatics

Les and Vampire T11 - Oakington

Members of 145 Course in Groundschool - Oakington 1960

5 FTS, Oakington - 1960. Les in front with some of 145 course

145 Course Wings Day - August 1960 - Les front row 2nd from right

Refuelling a 45 Sqn Canberra B2

Canberra Crew:- 'Digger' Balding, Les Warren, Jimmy Milne –
1962

B2 of 45 Sqn - On a bombing run

USAF B57 - Canberra US built under licence

Les Transport - RAF Tengah - 1961

45 Sqn lineup - Canberra B15, RAF Tengah

Loading 2" rockets in underwing pod on Canberra B15

Landing gear problem - RAF Tengah, Singapore - January 1963

Left main gear stuck up

Rocket rail kept wingtip off the ground thus preventing swing to left

Amourer making Ejector seats safe

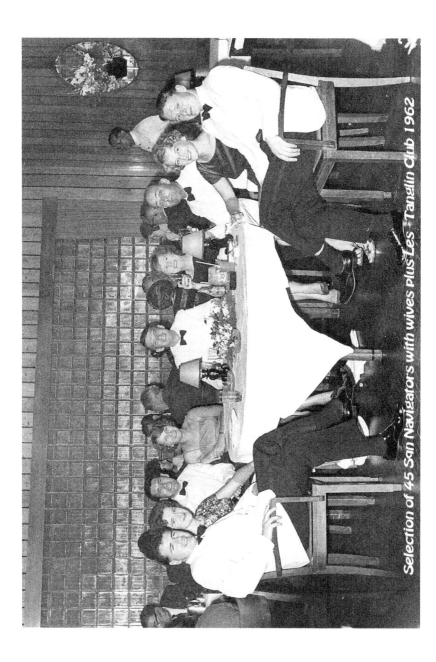

Selection of 45 San Navigators with wives plus Les - Tanglin Club 1962

CENTRAL FLYING SCHOOL

This is to Certify *that*

Fg. Off. L. C. Warren

has successfully graduated from the

Central Flying School

as a Qualified Flying Instructor

DATE *25. March 1964.*

H Bird-Wilson Air Cdre. COMMANDANT

Flt. Lt. Les Warren - checking log book - ULAS 1964

Chipmunk T1 - White Waltham - 1964

Spray from Vic Falls - Livingstone 1966

Victoria Falls

Victoria Falls - Zambia Side

Elephants crossing Zambesi

Party in the ZAF Officers' Mess - 1968

Well Dead Black Mamba
ZAF Livingstone 1969

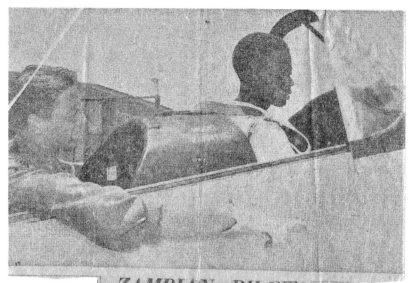

ZAMBIAN PILOT

ZAF pilot-in-training, Cadet L. P. Lemba receives flying instruction in a Chipmunk aircraft from Flight Lieutenant L. C. Warren at the Zambia Air Force Base at Livingstone. When qualified, Cadet Lemba will be among the first Zambians to be promoted to the rank of pilot officer.

Syphoning! Dealing with petrol rationing.

DH Beaver, Livingstone 1968

BOAC VC10 over Mt. Fuji, Japan

Dawn Departure - BOAC VC10

VC10 Taking Off

BOAC 747 Classic

B747 Classic

BA 747 Classic - on the ground at Vancouver, BC

SFO Les Warren

Ready for flight

SFO Les Warren - In Flight
B747 Classic - 1986

Co-Plt SFO Les Warren
Flt Deck of 747 Classic

Flt Engineer
Dave Bard

Les before leaving home
on first trip as Captain

British Airways B757

Pre - Flight Walkaround Inspection
B747-400

Preparing For Flight
BA 747-400

Refuelling a B747-400

Refuelling BA 747-400

BA B747-400 Preparing for Service

Pre-Flight Activity aound BA 747-400

Captain Les - B747-400
1991

Capt Les Warren & SFO Ray Coates
Flight Deck of B747-400, 1991

Ready to start
Les on 747-400

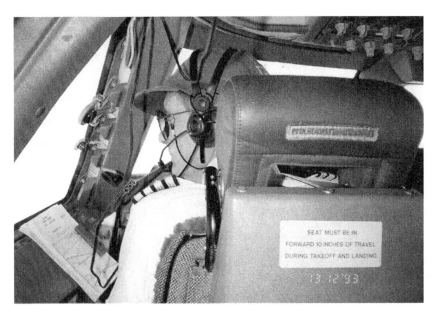

PUSH HEADREST UPTO RAISE

SEAT MUST BE IN
FORWARD 10 INCHES OF TRAVEL
DURING TAKEOFF AND LANDING

13 12 '93

Les appearing on Channel 7 with presenter Ann Sanders (Australia)

AEF Cadet in Tutor T1

Air Cadets - Ready for Flight

AEF Bulldog

AEF Chipmunk T1

6 AEF Pilots in front of Tutor T1 - RAF Benson
Les second from left

ABOUT THE AUTHOR

Les Warren

Les joined the RAF in 1958 at the age of 17 and signed up for a 12 year commission in the General Duties Branch of the service, training as a pilot. During his career in the RAF he spent time in Singapore, where he flew the Canberra twin jet bomber on 45 Sqn. and subsequently became a qualified flying instructor. As a QFI he served at RAF White Waltham instructing on the London University Air Squadron and subsequently on loan service in Zambia for 4 years.

After leaving the RAF he joined BOAC as a civil pilot flying the VC10, the Boeing 747 in the newly formed British Airways and then the Boeing 757, finally finishing his career on the 747-400. During the final years in BA and into retirement he flew as a RAF Reserve pilot in Air Experience Flights which were set up to give Air Cadets flying experience.

Since retiring from flying he lives with his wife near Woking.

AFTERWORD

If you've enjoyed this book or found it interesting, please take a minute to leave a review on Amazon.

Thank you.

Rita with her captain - Durban Christmas 1995

Printed in Great Britain
by Amazon